"I've had the distinct honor to serve with Jake Polumbo, Rob Polumbo, Chad Franks, and Larry Martin for the past 45 years while we were on active duty in the United States Air Force and now in the public business sector. Each is an exceptional 'baptized by fire' leader with firsthand experience on how to motivate people while driving an organization to greater heights. Simply stated, their stories and the real-world experiences they share in *Leadership at 100 Feet* are recipes for success ... these four warrior-leaders nailed it! Jake's description of 'near rocks, far rocks, lead, check six' and his brother Rob's 'Six Ps for success' are amazing lessons for any leader to apply in their professional and personal lives. Likewise, Chad's 'CARE' analogy and Larry's 'CONCEPT OF COMMAND' insights are nuggets of wisdom I wish I had learned much earlier in my life. Most importantly, each of these leaders does a brilliant job of drawing out the 'so what' lessons learned that superiors and leaders from all professional walks of life could practically apply. If you are interested in becoming a better boss, leader, friend, or family member, as well as being an integral part of an organizational climate and culture that is healthy and thriving, then this book is a must-read for you and the folks you serve with! As a former CEO of a veterans and first responder non-profit support organization, I would have bought copies of this book for each of my teammates!

Good hunting and as Jake says ... 'Check Six.'"

Robin Rand

General (Ret), United States Air Force
Commander, Air Force Global Stike Command,
Jul 2015 – Aug 2018

LEADERSHIP AT 100 FEET

GROWING LEADERS IN HIGH-PERFORMANCE TEAMS

CHAD FRANKS LARRY MARTIN
H.D. "JAKE" POLUMBO ROB POLUMBO

Edited and compiled by Julia L. Martin, APR; and Effective Project Management, Inc.

Introduction written by Todd Dantzler, Managing Director, SVN Saunders Ralston Dantzler Real Estate.

Cover design by: Effective Project Management, Inc.

ISBN: 9798376066843

Library of Congress Control Number: 2023903000

"Leaders should concentrate on being significant to those they lead so their success will live on long after they leave the organization."

Chad Franks

Major General (Ret), United States Air Force

INTRODUCTION

When these four Air Force generals asked me to write the introduction for this book titled *Leadership at 100 Feet,* I was incredibly honored and, to be honest, a little intimidated. Jake, Mumbles, Larry, and Sparky are four of the most accomplished people I personally know. I even grew up, competed in sports, and graduated high school in our hometown of Winter Haven, Florida, with Jake. His brother Mumbles graduated with my younger brother Brad.

All of these general officers are so incredibly accomplished in their active duty and reserve careers. Let me run some numbers for you. These officers combined for over 130 years in leadership positions. Two have led large "numbered" Air Forces, two worked at the Pentagon multiple times, one commanded MacDill Air Force Base in Tampa, Florida, and all have flown combat missions. Two piloted F-16 fighters, one flew C-130s and later commanded a KC-135 squadron, one flew MH/HH-60G special ops/rescue missions all over the world, and one even flew 21 combat missions as a general officer in the U-2 spy plane. Three of them graduated from the US Air Force Academy, and all told, they have accumulated thousands of flight hours and commanded and led many more thousands of troops for decades. They're a fun group of leaders, trust me, and all of them like a shot of "Jerimiah Weed" bourbon—once in a while.

Leadership at 100 Feet was born out of a desire for these so-called "Aces" to tell the story of their careers in the Air Force, the leadership lessons learned along the way, and the relationships that came from decades of service.

My father and uncles also served in our military and were honorably discharged, but I never served, and that is one reason why these stories and leadership lessons resonate with me. My life as a civilian has taken me down many leadership paths both in college and in my professional life, but I never had to display the discipline and dedication these gentlemen did over their entire careers.

After college, I joined my father's real estate company and entered the "chain of command" in my local Realtor association. I became president of that local association when I was 31 and, from there, moved up in the ranks of the Florida Realtors, becoming, at the time, the youngest president in their long and important history.

When I first became interested in leadership opportunities at Florida Realtors, I sought out some of the current leaders in the organization and told them I wanted to be involved. A man named RJ Collins, the president at that time, recognized my potential and commitment to our profession and became my mentor and close friend. He was able to put me on strategic task forces, important committees, and Presidential Advisory Groups, where my leadership experiences began to expand until I reached the pinnacle of becoming Florida Realtors President at age 40. RJ gave insight into the politics of leadership in a volunteer organization and showed me how to navigate its complexities to eventually become president in 2000. It was a great honor to do so, and like these four generals, I refined my leadership style by watching my mentor and others operate in complicated situations.

In 2010 I was elected and subsequently re-elected in 2014 by the majority of citizens in my county as one of five county commissioners. My public service on the commission included two four-year terms, with two years as the Chair of the Board. This was an interesting foray into political leadership with meetings that were not only held in public but were recorded and even broadcast live on public television. I was able to use the technical and personal skills I developed as a leader in Florida Realtors to become a better public servant, to be accountable to the people I led, and, ultimately, I learned how to take a larger view of my community. You'll learn more about accountability later in the book.

All along the way, I have been fortunate to have mentors and well-meaning folks around me to help me be a successful leader. And that is how I want you to utilize this book. It is filled with interesting, first-hand accounts of four successful general officers who have taught, mentored, and led men and women in difficult and challenging situations. Be it a small squadron, or a major command in the US Air Force, these Aces have done it. There are a few key points at the end of each chapter to help you with potential situations in your organization for people you're developing for future leadership positions.

I also suggest you pay particular attention to the lessons

learned in the last chapter of each author's section. These "takeaways" can form a roadmap for your organization, business, church, or even your family and include how to effectively manage and lead in today's tumultuous world. Some common themes you'll read about in these "final chapters" are the importance of role models; being flexible in your approach to identifying and guiding emerging leaders; analyzing and evaluating your team; striving for constant improvement of your team; and developing diverse leadership to avoid groupthink within your organization. You will also see how each created a sense of unity and commitment in their teams by knowing and respecting the members personally and professionally and always being accountable to them and the organization.

One lesson I learned over my lifetime of service is this: when you are in charge, it is your responsibility to identify your replacement. Not necessarily for the following year, as they are often already in the queue, but perhaps a few years out. Whether you mentor and coach them into positions to shine and develop as leaders or steer them on a path to academic and technical success, it is your responsibility to do so.

I hope you enjoy reading this book as much as I did. It will become a great tool for you to use for folks you are mentoring and training for leadership.

THE STORIES

PART 1

LARRY MARTIN

RETIRED MAJOR GENERAL LARRY MARTIN is a senior consultant with Two Blue Aces, LLC. Major General Martin retired in 2017, after 32 years of active service in the US Air Force. Prior to his military retirement, General Martin served as the Assistant Deputy Under Secretary of the Air Force, where he oversaw 226 Washington DC-based employees managing Air Force international matters with the United States Government, industry partners, and over 100 worldwide air forces.

"This is a hands-on book on applied leadership. The writing feels as if we are sitting on a back deck having a conversation one-on-one. Leadership is not bells and whistles. It's what you do every day. This book explains what that looks like and the mental focus of the leader to get it done. Regardless of the situation, this book helps a leader lead."

Dr. Bob Rohrlack, CCE

President and CEO, Tampa Bay Chamber

CHAPTER 1

LEADERSHIP, INTEGRITY, AND THE RIGHT THING

WHEN MY FRIENDS and I talk about how to solve the world's problems, our discussions have a common refrain: we believe good leadership makes organizations successful. So, when we decided to write a book that reflected our passion, the topic was easy. The best leaders I know do simple things well—they have expertise in their field, they know how to take care of people, they possess integrity, and they build cultures in their organizations based on trust and accountability.

THE BEGINNING. Growing up in Minnetonka, west of Minneapolis, I just sort of always knew I would do something with airplanes. As a boy, I memorized every library book I could find on airplanes, especially military airplanes. By the time I was in junior high, I had decided the best way to fly those planes was to go to the Air Force Academy and be an Air Force pilot. I thought I was a good leader on sports teams, the band, and Boy Scouts, but when I entered the Air Force Academy on June 22, 1981, I began to see just how much more I had to learn.

At the Academy, I was immersed in an aviation culture and grew even more intense about being a pilot. During my junior year, a group of cadets and I visited Barksdale Air Force Base in Louisiana and stayed in the homes of families on base. Our host couple was a pair of Air Force nurses, male and female. At dinner, our female host asked our small group what we wanted to do in the Air Force. We all enthusiastically told her we wanted to be fighter pilots. She nodded at everyone but then thoughtfully looked at me and said: "Nah, you won't be a fighter pilot." Later that night, she privately came up to me, as I think I was visibly crushed by her comment and said: "Don't worry about not being a fighter pilot; you don't have the attitude to be one." It wasn't until much later that what she said really resonated. She saw that I did not have a fighter pilot's particular ego and drive and that I needed to be part of a crew.

Though I excelled as a cadet and was selected to go to pilot training, I did not do as well there as some of my other classmates. On assignment night, my lower class standing sent me to fly the "less desirable" C-130 at Little Rock AFB, Arkansas, and *that* turned out to be the best thing that ever happened to me.

While the nurse at Barksdale had been harsh as she assessed my fighter pilot peers, she was dead on about me—I did not have the right personality to fly a fighter. I did, however, have the right skills and demeanor to thrive in my new assignment as part of and later as a leader of a C-130 crew. I loved everything about the C-130 *Hercules*—its mission, its people, everything. If you ask my wife, she will grudgingly admit my first love was probably the C-130 (I met her in Little Rock, and she is the love of my life, my best friend, and ... the editor of this book.) The US Air Force has flown some version of the C-130 since 1954—it is indisputably the most successful and versatile aircraft ever flown. When I signed into the 50th Tactical Airlift Squadron (the "Red Devils") in 1986, my job entailed flying a variety of missions—from hauling cargo to runways paved and unpaved to airdropping people and cargo while flying in formation and single ship, day, and night everywhere in the world. And it was there, at my first squadron, in a 30+-year-old airplane, that I learned about leadership, integrity, working on a team, accountability and how to take care of people. And ... I loved it. (We'll talk more about how helping the folks you lead love what they do benefits them and your team.)

LEARNING LEADERSHIP AND INTEGRITY. As a young pilot, I learned about leadership by observing great leaders. I flew with some of the world's best pilots, masters of their craft. I respected them for their technical knowledge and proficiency, but as I discovered, being a great pilot did not necessarily translate into being a great leader. **The best aircraft commanders led both the people they directly commanded on their crew and the whole base team required to get the mission done.** As superior communicators, they marshaled everything needed to make the mission happen. They showed me how simply saying "thank you" could motivate people to work towards a difficult, common goal.

While a C-130 aircraft commander could order someone on the crew to do something, the best leaders led their crews by example and inspiration. They retained the ultimate responsibility for getting the mission done and made key decisions as needed. They depended on their crew members to functionally lead tasks (like the flight engineer for maintenance problems or the loadmaster for cargo on and off-load) and trusted their expertise. The best leaders realized their job revolved around taking care of their people, getting their people the resources they needed, and then ... getting out of the way.

I learned my most vivid lesson about integrity when I was selected as a Low Altitude Parachute Extraction System (LAPES) pilot, a special qualification for highly skilled crew members. LAPES was developed during the Vietnam Conflict to deliver large, heavy loads into very small bases without landing. It involved flying five feet above the ground and extending large parachutes behind the plane to extract 40,000 pounds of cargo out the rear door in two seconds. The mission's riskiest part came during the 15 to 20 seconds after we deployed the parachutes to extract the load, when the load literally exploded out the back of our airplane, dropped a few feet to the ground, and skidded to a stop. During those few seconds, each extraction chute billowed with enough drag to overpower one of our four engines—our biggest loads needed three and sometimes four parachutes. When all went according to plan, the system provided a reliable, even thrilling, way to get a lot of stuff to soldiers or Marines very quickly.

But everything did not always go as planned, and we trained hard to prepare for this. For most emergencies during standard C-130 missions, our actions were calm and considered. Very few emergency procedures were committed to memory and executed quickly (called "**BOLDFACE**" procedures for how they were printed in our checklists), and we jokingly said the first step of every emergency procedure was to "wind the clock." "Winding the clock" helped us slow down and evaluate the situation, identify the whole problem, and resolve the situation safely and correctly.

As we extracted our load five feet above the ground at 150 mph, we had fractions of a second to recognize any problem and react. We did not have time to "wind the clock," so as a LAPES crew member, you memorized every possible emergency procedure for the drop. In these situations, everything was a Boldface procedure. Never in my life had I been so immediately accountable to my crew mates—my actions in those fractions of a second might determine if we lived or died. We depended on and trusted each other, so we prepared hard, practiced repeatedly, and held everyone on the crew accountable. And as a part of that culture of integrity, if a crew member was not prepared and did not live up to standards, they were no longer allowed to do the LAPES mission.

Though the missions were demanding, I never had so much fun or found so much satisfaction in doing well on something that mattered so much. I had always been considered a good leader, and I truly enjoyed being part of a team, a band, a scout troop ... but the requirements for this mission meant so much more. My experience serving as part of a LAPES crew showed me how accountability formed the foundation for integrity. Being held accountable and having earned their trust made me proud to be part of and lead those crews.

DOING THE RIGHT THING EVERYWHERE. I believe integrity can be described as doing the right thing, even when no one is looking. On those LAPES missions, we depended on each other, so we studied, prepared, practiced, worked hard, and cut no corners. The instantaneous requirement to react when a mission went wrong meant that you were either prepared or you weren't—and if you weren't, you and your crew mates might die.

Not every leadership situation grabs a team's attention as starkly as a LAPES mission, so part of a leader's job is to build a culture based on integrity that holds everyone accountable. Great leaders set that expectation and hold team members to a high standard. And it doesn't matter if it is a real-world situation like flying a mission, a learning situation like sitting in a classroom planning for the future, or running a successful business. You always do the Right Thing.

CONCEPT OF COMMAND. A few years later, as a student at the Marine Corps Command and Staff College, my classmates and I prepared to lead larger teams like squadrons and battalions. As part of our studies, we wrote our "concept of command," a broadsheet to share with our units on what we held dear and what was important to us. My letter centered on the importance of integrity and teamwork. It read:

1. We will never compromise our integrity.
2. Each member of the team takes care of one another.
3. The best organizations function well as a team. When everyone works together to accomplish our mission, we all benefit, and we all have fun. If you do not plan to contribute to our success, I will do my best to remove you from our organization.
4. I believe that you are extraordinary people and will treat you in accordance with the "Big Boy/Girl Theory", i.e., you are men and women who know right from wrong. I will treat you as Big Boys and Girls until such time that you stop acting that way. If you prove me wrong, you will be disciplined. Period.
5. I believe commanders must listen to and learn from subordinates, but the buck stops with the commander.
6. Our job is to defend and serve our country. Although this often puts us at risk, our job is to manage that risk in daily, often dangerous operations and accomplish our mission in the safest manner possible.
7. The important things are always simple; the simple always hard.

I used this letter repeatedly throughout my career, modifying it slightly for the different organizations, units, and teams I led, but it remained remarkably consistent. I found from Day One it showed the type of team I wanted to lead and forged a healthy culture. We established a foundation of trust between every team member that we would tell the truth, take responsibility for our actions, and hold each other accountable. When we shared these key values, the team did not need me as the leader to always hold them responsible. Instead, they held each other to account—it was what we did.

TAKEAWAYS

- Leaders establish a climate of integrity and hold the team accountable.
- Leaders get the resources people need.

CHAPTER 2

THE CASE FOR NUMBER 2

> "We are outgunned, outmanned, outnumbered, outplanned. We gotta make an all out stand. Ayo, I'm gonna need a right-hand man."
> —George Washington, *Hamilton*

AND WITH THESE WORDS from Lin-Manuel Miranda's play *Hamilton*, George Washington makes a plea for someone to share his leadership load. Alexander Hamilton would become almost a son to Washington, serving as one of Washington's executive officers and filling his critical need for the nascent American Army.

Most leadership books focus on the CEO, the entrepreneur, or the commander as the leader, but few discuss how other leaders impact an organization. We are familiar with great No. 2's from literature and pop culture, be they Watson to Holmes, Spock to Kirk, or Hamilton to Washington. In these cases, mission and team demands exceed a single person's leadership capacity. The first officer, vice president, or deputy serves the team by addressing shortcomings, being a foil to the leader, and delivering what the team needs to succeed. The No. 2 must communicate extremely well, be adaptable, and be humble. He or she must focus on getting the job done, taking care of the team, as well as providing good counsel to the leader.

So, who does a good No. 2 work for? It's a flexible role that both works for the boss and takes care of the team to get its mission done. Several times in my Air Force career, I served as the No. 2 for large teams, and I was usually matched to a boss to help provide balance as part of a larger command team. If my boss was quiet, I might need to be an extrovert to help him or her communicate; if my boss was brusque, I needed to help the team better understand our direction more tactfully; if my boss needed to travel extensively, I was the stay-home presence. Some days I needed to be a strong presence; other days, I needed to fade into the background—and, most importantly, not make a fuss about being so flexible. While you work for the boss, you take care of the team and stay focused on the mission, all the while being humble. As the No. 2, you serve to help the team succeed and the leader lead, but it's not about you.

A great No. 2 is a great communicator. He or she relentlessly and ruthlessly communicates to build relationships, lessen tension, and solve problems. Communication drives everything. With the boss, the role requires flexibility to build trust and transparency. With the team, it requires diplomacy and clarity. If you work in the same space with your boss, you might find it easier to maintain touch points—meetings, calls, and one-on-one conversations. If your boss travels frequently or does business away from the home office, you must find a way to communicate and stay aligned. The things your boss wants to know will vary based on their leadership style and your organizational structure. In one job that required shift work, I mirrored what my boss did as he worked days, and I worked nights; we interfaced at shift change. For another boss who mostly worked on-site, I took on projects that needed the right horsepower; we spoke each day to share our progress. In a third job, my boss traveled internationally over 200 days a year; I sent her daily/weekly updates on normal business and called to discuss time-critical or sensitive issues. You must communicate with your boss to keep them comfortable and be flexible enough to adapt to their needs.

You must find the right balance in critical relationships with your boss' direct reports. Sometimes direct reports will come to you to find a way around the boss. I made it clear to direct reports that I worked for the boss and that I would not hide anything they told me from the boss. I often helped direct reports shape how they would inform the boss about an issue, coaching them to know what might be asked or have expected them to have already done. In those cases, I might tell the boss that the direct report was coming to them with an issue, but I always had the direct report carry the water—I felt they needed to build a relationship with the boss. If the direct report did not want to inform the boss, I let them know I would keep the boss informed. I built trust with direct reports as part of my role to teach, mentor, and lead—they knew they could come to me for advice, but we never forgot who we worked for.

Not all leader/No. 2 relationships work well. Insecure leaders might consider their deputy to be a competitor. Overly ambitious deputies can overstep their roles as a No. 2. The insecure leader might try to isolate their deputy, keeping them in the dark about critical decisions. The ambitious No. 2 might work without the leader's awareness inside and outside the team to assert his or her authority. These contentious relationships can fracture a team into cliques that undermine performance, destroy morale, and detract from the mission. When the leader or the No. 2 surprise each other, distrust follows. Not every relationship works, but the best partnerships depend on great communication.

THE IMPORTANCE OF TRUST. Senior leader relationships depend on trust, the faith built between people that each will do the right thing. Transparency builds on basic communication and reinforces trust by revealing each party's decision-making process. Transparency also helps manage expectations by keeping everyone aware of what is and is not possible.

The leader I worked for, who traveled extensively, had great trust in me and her direct reports to execute our mission. On several occasions, I could tell on our weekly phone calls when her level of concern and anxiety went up about an issue. In every case, our lack of communication caused the tension—whether it was my fault for not keeping her informed or her busy schedule prevented her from keeping aligned. As the No. 2, you must remember your boss bears ultimate responsibility for the team's success and failure, and your job is to help the leader and the team succeed. As a result, I needed to step up my communications to be more transparent to keep the boss comfortable, aligned with current events, and included in key decisions. I also needed to talk with my boss to understand how I had raised her concern. Was I sending the wrong kind of updates? Did we need to call and talk more? Was there an issue we had missed? Those follow-up discussions increased trust and transparency and prevented potential conflicts.

Impatient, impetuous No. 2's often do not trust their boss and think they need to be the smarter of the two to keep the mission moving. Again, the key here is to rely on each other and share information since, very often, the leader will have more information about relationships or objectives than he or she can share. A commander once told me if I came into his office one day, I might find him wrestling a bear, kicking his butt, and he might ask me to "help the bear." He told me to trust him and help the bear, even if helping the bear went against my every instinct. When I asked why I should help the bear, my boss told me that he might need to "let the bear win" to advance a greater need for our team—helping him beat the bear (blindly) would hurt our team. He taught me a critical lesson about trust—he might not have time (or the willingness) to tell me everything, but I needed to trust him, and he would trust me to follow his lead.

A great No. 2 also knows when and when not to step up to be the leader. The range of decisions made in the leader's absence comes down to how much risk is involved. Routine, day-to-day low-risk decisions can be made without consulting the leader. With greater risk and exposure comes greater consequences, so the leash gets shorter, and the leader needs to be involved. Just how long of a leash depends a lot on how much trust exists between the leader and the No. 2—more trust allows for less oversight. Although each relationship and situation will be different, trust and transparency will always be the key. If the unit leader's duties place large demands on their time to represent the team on the outside, then the leader should empower the team, especially the No. 2, to build parameters for decisions in his or her absence. If not, you risk dragging work to a stop every time you leave the office.

THERE ARE ALWAYS TWO SIDES *(OR MORE).* I got to see how good relationships work from both sides. One day, while serving as second-in-command at the largest U.S. air base in the Middle East, my boss was occupied with a major conference, and after landing, a B-1 bomber lost hydraulic pressure and brakes. The aircraft veered off the taxiway into a ditch before catching fire and becoming fully engulfed in flame, and its full bomb load began to explode. For the previous year, my boss worked to prepare our team (and especially me) to deal with a crisis. We worked hard to prepare emergency responses, and our work paid off that night. While we waited on our commander's return, the team quickly took action to rescue the crew and protect our base, and when he arrived, he knew immediately we had done the right thing by executing the emergency protocols without missing a beat. Despite a horrific fire that consumed the aircraft, the crew survived, and we returned the base to operations the next day.

When I was base commander at MacDill Air Force Base, I took my family on a trip up the East coast for some time off. When I called back to the base that first night to ask my deputy, Colonel Dave Cohen, a question, my office told me he was in the base command post handling a situation that affected not only the base, but national security as well. When I called the command post, I was told Colonel Cohen could not talk because he was briefing the White House on the situation. I calmly asked the command post chief to have my deputy call me when he was done, but only when he had enough time. I knew he would do the right thing to protect our team and the base. Dave was a great No. 2 who knew when to step up, and I slept well that night—despite the threat to our base.

TAKEAWAYS

A great No. 2:

- Serves the team and the leader.
- Communicates relentlessly and ruthlessly to build trust and transparency.
- Knows when to step up or not.

CHAPTER 3

LEADING AN INTERNATIONAL ORGANIZATION: BUILDING TRUST WITH TRANSPARENCY AND PERSISTENCE

> "Geography has made us neighbors. History has made us friends. Economics has made us partners, and necessity has made us allies. Those whom God has so joined together, let no man put asunder."
> —John F. Kennedy

MY THOUGHTS on leadership have focused so far on trust. When conducting military operations, complexity grows as you add partners. The simplest operations are those done by a single team from one service, but today's high-threat environments mean we usually fight with other services in joint operations. Complexity grows when we add international allies and partners. Though we trust our own team, we are naturally skeptical about those on the outside, whether they be from other services, countries, or just down the hall. Building trust requires leaders to articulate a common, shared purpose nurtured by transparent and persistent connections.

BUILDING TRUST EVEN WHEN COMPETING. Building trust starts with simple relationships like the one between two brothers. Over the past three years, I have had the honor of commissioning not one but both of my sons into military service. Now, my sons are very different people. My Space Force Guardian prefers suits and ties and Sperry's; my Army Soldier prefers shorts and tees and Birkenstocks—with socks. One came into his military service after being a international defense journalist and television host; the other had been (and still is) an excellent multi-sport athlete. Though different in culture and style, they love and trust one another and would lay down their lives for the other—but not without a little "smack" talk thrown in. The younger outranks his older brother by exactly 364 days, a fact that comes up daily. Their competition only intensifies when they compare their training (you had it so easy!), pick at each other's uniforms (Bro, you look like Spock), and question the sanity of the path they chose. As an Air Force veteran, I find their exchanges enlightening ... and amusing.

While watching their (mostly) good-natured banter, I saw the pride and competition I have seen across the military with people and groups who should automatically trust each other, and work together but sometimes fall short. Team pride can be good-natured and positive as it builds esprit de corps and resilience. But rejecting people outside our group, who do not look or think like us, can sow distrust, cripple the mission, and crush our most important asset, our people. The key to overcoming these divisions depends on building trust and transparency.

DIVERSITY AS STRENGTH AND AS WEAKNESS. The diversity found in our military provides great strength but has the potential to be a barrier to success. From an organizational perspective, our military branches can be complex, stove-piped, and clannish. Look at our uniforms: we rightly have pride in patches and badges, insignia designed to highlight the diverse groups within the services that carry deep meaning about our training, history, and traditions. Sometimes these differences result in the lighthearted, (mostly) positive banter and competition I see in my sons, but sometimes it becomes intensely negative. As a result, we may think those outside our tribe or service are wrong, incompetent, and even evil. When groups and cultures clash and communication lines break down, tensions rise. Add in the complex issues we see in modern society related to religion, race, gender, sexual identity, and political viewpoints, and a team that is supposed to get along sometimes has challenges getting the mission done. Then, add in different languages, cultural values, and national aspirations on an international mission, and the degree of difficulty and opportunity for challenges multiplies quickly.

Yet, successful organizations depend on the varied opinions, outlooks, and experiences that every member of the team (and some outside the team) provides to solve challenging issues. We must see these different points of view as a positive and believe everyone has something to bring to the table. During the global COVID-19 pandemic, companies, organizations, and their people answered the challenges by being flexible and innovative. Work from home? Shift our business model? OK, let us get together as a team and find a way. And on both sides, there must be trust: can we, the employer, trust you, the employees, to work from home and get the job done? Can we, the employees, trust you, the employer, to let us be part of the solution as we shift our business? And these changes come amid a shifting demographic landscape where our workforce is growing more diverse. As I see it, leaders can see our country's dynamic workforce as a hindrance or embrace it as a tool to unlock opportunities for larger markets, discover innovative solutions, drive costs down, and build a future that not only works NOW but is also sustainable. So how does a diverse team succeed? It depends on that foundation of trust.

THERE'S THAT ISSUE OF TRUST AGAIN... Creating the trust your team needs to succeed, both internally and externally, depends equally on articulating a common, shared purpose and must be earned through transparent, persistent relationships. In the military, we saw much of our conflict grow when we were at home, simply training. During those times, we found it easy to criticize other parts of our team. We found the most cohesiveness when we deployed and shared a common mission across units and services. As we worked closer together, the mission united us and lifted us above petty conflicts. Even though we had a common purpose, we still sometimes mistrusted those "others," but our proximity allowed us to overcome our issues through transparency and persistence.

While stationed at the Pentagon and working with our international partners, I learned firsthand about the power of earning trust through transparency and persistence. As part of an amazing team of Air Force international affairs professionals who spoke our partner's languages and valued their cultures, I plunged into a world where we worked close relationships with over 100 air forces daily. The representatives of these air forces owed THEIR allegiance to THEIR particular national interests, THEIR national goals, and, like us, THEIR own values and biases. So how did we find common ground with a group this diverse? We built upon long-standing bedrock relationships that had well-defined goals and purposes, like those we share with our NATO allies or with Pacific partners in Australia, Japan, and the Republic of Korea. We also explored newer relationships with states formerly aligned with the Soviet bloc and in India as its stance allowed talks with the United States and built a common purpose together.

Our partners made important, sensitive requests for technology transfers, shared training, and cooperative research through our team. They wanted to partner and share with the best Air Force in the world. To build trust, our Air Force team made a commitment to transparency with our partners. We did our best to fully understand what our partner wanted, to make sure the request was heard by the United States Government and did our utmost to help them get what they wanted. We gave them honest feedback about their request and as much transparency about the process as we could. While we made it clear we worked for the United States Air Force, we focused on finding the right way to say yes.

Yet, by the difficult nature of their requests, sometimes with little or no explanation from us, we had to tell our partners no. We consistently and persistently made it clear we were saying no to the request, **not the relationship**. The trust we built with our partners allowed us to continue working collaboratively. On many occasions, I told our closest allies that the United States could not meet their request and then, the next day, asked our ally for something on our behalf. The commitment and persistence we showed for these relationships demonstrated to our partners that we wanted a long-term relationship, not just a quick transaction. Through trust, through persistent, transparent communication, and a common purpose, we overcame our disagreements, and our relationships flourished.

TRUST IS TRUST IS TRUST. Whether in an international, organizational, or brotherly relationship, building trust requires leaders to articulate a common, shared purpose nurtured by transparent and persistent connections.

TAKEAWAYS

Building trust in an international organization depends upon:

- Defining a common, shared purpose
- Building transparent, persistent relationships
- Trust can be seen when you can say no to the request but remain committed to the relationship.

CHAPTER 4
DOING THE RIGHT THING

"With great power comes great responsibility."
—Uncle Ben, *Spiderman*

WHAT DO SUPERHEROES have to do with it? What would you say is your superpower as a leader and as a person? What attribute makes you more successful, a better leader, and a better part of your community and family? When you get down to basics, superheroes share the same superpower. You can take away their x-ray vision, frozen breath, golden bracelets, super strength, and cool gadgets, and at the end of the day, superheroes can be trusted to back up each other and the world. They have character and act with integrity. They rise above great adversity (even Kryptonite) and sacrifice what they hold dear to do the right thing.

While the dictionary tells us that integrity is "the quality of being honest and having strong moral principles," I use a simpler definition of having character and acting with integrity. "Do the right thing when no one is looking." And I believe doing the right thing, living, and acting with character and integrity is the best path for you, your team, and your customers.

APPLICATION COMES FROM WITHIN. You don't ***practice*** learning character and integrity like you would playing the piano or hitting a golf ball. You ***apply*** character and integrity in your daily life. Character and integrity are attributes that are inherently part of someone, not a discrete skill you can pick up at just about any point in your life. Character grows and develops from experiences and culture, from role models and situations, and from a broad sense of who we are. It lives inside us. I might decide to learn a new backhand in just a few weeks, but altering my character takes longer and requires something more significant.

We develop character by observing, watching, and learning from those around us. As I grew up, I was lucky to have great role models like my parents, coaches, teachers, and Scout leaders who did the right things, made the right choices, and were accountable, humble, and transparent.

ROLE MODELS—DEVELOPING AND BUILDING CHARACTER. I grew up a history nut and later taught history at the Air Force Academy. I believe studying history serves as an aircraft simulator for life. My early heroes were Ulysses Grant, George Marshall, Bernard Schriever, Harry Truman, and John Kennedy. While the early images I held of my heroes were very one-dimensional and idealized, later, I grew to admire them more as I read deeply and learned more. Each of my heroes had deep personal flaws and wrestled with tough ethical choices and did not always prevail. As I thought about their choices and the actions they took, and the mistakes they made, I built a sense of right and wrong.

Faced with tough ethical choices, we often know what to do in our "gut," even if we know that doing the right thing might be hard. As a leader, I found I could trust my gut feeling about the most important questions and act based on that feeling. The only time I lost sleep was when I deviated from those feelings. And not surprisingly, the only times I was wrong was when I did not trust my gut.

When we find ourselves in stressful situations, we get to use the character we have developed during our life. Our decisions reveal our character. Nearly 40 years ago, I went to the Air Force Academy. For most of us cadets, the trials, and tribulations of our first year were not so much about ***learning*** character but about ***revealing*** character while dealing with tough situations. Yes, we all had more to learn, and the rigors of Academy life helped us strengthen and refine our character. We lived under the "Cadet Honor Code," where cadets promise "to not lie, cheat nor steal, nor tolerate those among them who do so." We were taught that we never let our wingman down, to never leave them behind, and to hold each other accountable. Those attributes practiced at the

Air Force Academy are the foundation of our Air Force culture.

Across 40 years of service, I watched warriors hold each other accountable. Why do Soldiers, Sailors, Marines, Airmen, and Guardians fight? They initially might fight for ideology, patriotism, or religion, but as the conflict continues, they end up fighting for each other. Their sense of accountability becomes a core value. They would rather die than let their wingman, battle buddy, shipmate, or teammate down. I have been moved by the determination our wounded warriors show by working hard at recovery so they can go back with their team and finish the mission.

KEY RELATIONSHIPS AND DECISION MAKING. Character, integrity, and accountability should matter, even if you do not have to make life-and-death decisions every day. Here's how they might apply to three key relationships you have in your business. First, you have a responsibility to your customers. Your customers want to put their trust in you. They want to trust your competence and your character. If you take an ethical shortcut in getting or servicing a customer, you will likely be caught, either in the short term or even worse, after establishing a long history of doing wrong. I'm not a fan of doing anything that would lead to losing a license, earning censure, or worse, going to jail.

Second, you also have a responsibility to your team. You should care about character as you build your team. A lack of trust and accountability creates a toxic environment. Do your employees see a leader who takes ethical shortcuts or treats people poorly? Do they observe toxic teammates who put self before the team, get away with it, and get promoted? As we have seen during times with tight labor markets, employees have options and will not tolerate a toxic workplace for long. And even if you have the right values of character and integrity, you will have to help members of your team learn and apply them. A critical role that you have as a leader is to establish the organization's culture by reinforcing the right messages. Some on your team might confuse hitting the immediate metric or doing anything to win with the greater importance of acting with good character and integrity. Your leadership will help them understand how your team values integrity. If they can't or won't understand and live up to your team's culture, then you should help them find another place to work.

Finally, you have a responsibility to yourself. Ultimately, you sell goods and services to solve a customer's need or challenge. In today's transparent market, your unscrupulous actions will be discovered, and everyone will know. Isn't that bad for your business and your reputation? YES! It comes down to your good name, your reputation, your business, and your team. Your character and integrity are your superpowers and your foundation. If you lose them, you have nothing!

HOW DO WE GET THERE? So, let's talk about some practical steps you can take in your business or organization to build this foundation of character and integrity. You must establish a culture that values and practices character, forge your team, and establish a long-term foundation.

Start to build your culture by sharing your expectations. I used my "Concept of Command" (Chapter 1) throughout my career to help explain my expectations, modifying it slightly for the different organizations, units, and teams I led, but it remained remarkably consistent. I found that it established from Day One the type of team I wanted to lead and forged a healthy culture from the start. Our team could accept and learn from mistakes made with good intent, but we could not, and we would not, tolerate failures of integrity.

While a written affirmation of your expectations may be important, your actions speak much louder than your words. You must demonstrate your own accountability and your trust in the team. During my time as a wing commander, members of my staff offered to help with a personal task, and I accepted. An observant junior staff member asked if this was proper, and I realized I was wrong, and she was right. Though I had stressed to my team the importance of raising issues like this immediately, she still displayed courage in doing so. I brought my whole team into my office, apologized for my mistake, took measures to ensure we did not repeat the same mistake again and praised her for bringing the issue to my attention. You thank a teammate like her and ensure your team knows you expect them to act the same way. No leader is perfect, and your team not only sees your faults very clearly but expects you to acknowledge those faults just like any teammate. By holding yourself accountable, you build trust over suspicion and establish the right practices.

AND THAT BRINGS US BACK TO CHARACTER. To forge your team, choose your teammates carefully and always pick people with good character and integrity. Given the choice between a stellar performer with a poor character reputation and an average performer with impeccable character, who would you choose for your team? Remember, character is an attribute learned over a lifetime. You can train skills, but overcoming bad attributes is extremely hard.

Once bad attributes get a foothold in your organization, they are very hard to root out. When doing wrong becomes normal and acceptable, correcting bad attributes takes a powerful paradigm shift. Be aware of what author Simon Sinek calls "ethical fading" in his 2019 book, *The Infinite Game*. This is a condition in a culture that "allows people to act in unethical ways in order to advance their own interests, often at the expense of others, while falsely believing that they have not compromised their own moral principles." If someone has poor character, you can make them leave the team, but realize their influence may live on.

While individuals might change their path relatively quickly, changing an organization's culture takes much longer. My Air Force Academy mentor, Colonel Martin "Joe" Johansen, was a retired Air Force fighter pilot whose father was a cavalry officer in the famed 9th and 10th Cavalry, the "Buffalo Soldiers." Joe's father told him that rooting out bad leadership in a unit took four years for every year of bad leadership. Junior leaders trained by bad leaders had to be retrained, refocused, and a better culture had to be established. Overcoming bad leadership takes persistence and determination to establish the long-term foundation your team needs.

REPUTATION MATTERS. Your goal is to build a great long-term reputation. It takes hard work and time. You can ruin a reputation built by a thousand good interactions with just one ethical failure. Partnerships were hard to build, fragile if violated, and the bedrock of how you play a long game with your team, your customers, and the person you see in the mirror.

Acting with character and integrity won't solve every issue for you. It won't write your business plan or market your company—these challenges require your innovation, your savvy, and ultimately, your grit. Doing the right thing will build the trust you and your team need to weather hard times and grow for the long-term. THIS is your superpower! Use it!

TAKEAWAYS

- Character and Integrity build, sustain, and remain the foundation of your life and business; they are key to your relationships with customers, employees, family, community, and self.
- Once in place, changing an organization's bad culture takes huge time and effort.

CHAPTER 5

MENTORING AND OPPORTUNITIES–STEPPING OFF THE BEATEN PATH

WHEN WE LOOK in the mirror on our most successful days, humble people know we do not achieve success alone. We depend on family, friends, bosses, and teammates to help. If you were like me growing up, you observed, watched, and learned. I was lucky to have great role models—they did the right things, made the right choices, were accountable, transparent, sacrificed, and almost always humble. Were you?

Taking care of your organization's people and developing them for the future is a critical leadership task, possibly the most important task a leader faces. Successful entry-level leaders must possess technical competence in their field, excellent professionalism, and a passion for getting the mission done. Senior leaders must grow their own skill set to include the tools needed to develop their people. Whether growing someone to eventually replace you as the leader or helping everyone on the team reach their full potential, great leaders always ***build their team***.

TAKING CARE OF YOUR PEOPLE AND YOUR TEAM. I served as the senior leader talent manager for one of the Air Force's major commands and served under General John Handy, the Air Mobility Command Commander, as we helped him select and develop his best colonels to become general officers. I worked closely with his Eighteenth Air Force commander, Lieutenant General William Welser III, who oversaw nearly twenty installations and wings. I learned a lot from both commanders about the demands of senior leadership in large organizations.

As Lieutenant General Welser considered his promotion rankings for his installation and wing commanders, he expressed some frustration to me and my deputy, Captain Bill Fischer, about how to differentiate a slate of excellent leaders as they were selected to be a general officer. The leaders in the promotion pool had risen to a high level based on their technical competence, professionalism, and passion. Cheekily, we offered to do a possible ranking for his consideration, and he sent us on our way to draft the list. Within thirty minutes, we dropped the list on his desk. An hour later, he came to my office, threw the list on my desk, and said: "I would swap #6 and #7—otherwise, your list matched mine; now explain to me how you built it."

His first thought was that we had seen some correspondence between him and General Handy. I assured him we had not seen anything like that, but we had a pretty good idea of what Handy and he valued in their people. In fact, we hoped our ranking reflected what we had learned from them. I explained how we built our ratings based on three factors:

- First, we had a basic idea of how the leaders performed.
- Second, we observed how well each leader knew the Air Force personnel system and how they took care of and mentored their people. We gave the leaders who understood the system and were the most involved in their people's success the highest rankings.
- And finally, we observed how those senior leaders treated the superb young personnel manager who worked across the office from me. Those who treated her rudely or dismissed her out-of-hand quickly fell to the bottom of our list. We heard every phone call they made to her—remember, integrity is doing the right thing when nobody's looking.

Fischer and I realized that leaders, especially senior leaders, must be people-focused superstars. A leader's business is the mission, and the number one factor driving success is the team's people. Those leaders who valued and took the best care of their people usually had the teams that did the mission best.

MENTORING FOR MUTUAL BENEFIT. Developing your team members comes back to building trust and transparency in your team and helps you create mutual benefits for the person and the team. In the Air Force, we clearly tell our people that mission comes first, but we always take care of our people the best we can. Some leaders do not take the time to develop great team members, perhaps fearing that they will leave for better jobs or will try to take the leader's job. In a large organization like the Air Force, I knew my people would be part of my team for a finite period and my responsibility was to prepare them for greater responsibility and leadership further on in their careers. Today's mobile workforce can make it harder to justify investing time and effort in your employees, but companies that work to find a mutual benefit for the employee and the organization will have the best culture, the best retention, and the best performance.

When new arrivals came to my organization, I met with them for a one-on-one interview. We discussed the organization, our mission, our heritage, our expectations, and where that person fits in. We also discussed their goals, their background, their family, and any concerns. When we discussed the future, I asked each Airman to consider what they wanted to do, like upgrade to instructor, cross-train to another career field, become a squadron commander, or even find a civilian career when their Air Force commitment time was done. We did an exercise where I asked them to write down three possible futures and outline a plan that got them to those futures. Their plan included milestones based on their family plans, education desires, future assignments, and anything else that mattered to them. I asked them to come back to me in a month to discuss the plan, but only after they had discussed it with their spouse, significant other, or another person they considered important in their life.

Together, we built realistic plans that balanced the team's needs and the member's wishes to find mutual benefit. When we met again, we discussed the way ahead and how the Air Force, our team, and I could help each person achieve their goal. I used the meetings to help make the Air Force's personnel process and development goals more transparent to our people and their families to help set reasonable expectations all around. Many spouses thanked me for having their partner come home to discuss what the future might hold and appreciated the chance to understand and make an input. The discussions fostered better questions all around as we built a plan centered on trust and transparency.

DEVELOPING AND RETAINING DIVERSE TALENTS.

"I shall be telling this with a sigh
Somewhere ages and ages hence:
Two roads diverged in a wood, and I—
I took the one less traveled by,
And that has made all the difference."
—Robert Frost, *The Road Not Taken*

In a flying unit, career plans often looked similar and revolved around upgrades to aircraft commander, instructor, evaluator, and job progressions inside the squadron and on to the group, wing, major command, and Pentagon staff billets. Stepping off the well-worn path was considered risky and often just sidetracked someone from reaching squadron command and beyond at the same time as their peers.

After my initial six years flying the handsome, high-winged, high-performance C-130 *Hercules*, I received a call from the Air Force Academy History Department asking me if I would consider returning to get a master's degree and teach at the Academy, a detour that would take me off a normal career path for over five years. Definitely not a mainstream choice and definitely not what the hard-charging career-minded pilot would do. But I had the skills and the desire to teach and mentor future leaders, and I realized I could make a positive difference for the Air Force that mattered to me. I took the offer and stepped off the "normal" career track by attending the Academy. I was ready to accept the career consequences of the detour, and I was the only one in that year's cohort of 17 instructor pilots who took the unusual path of teaching at the Academy.

While studying for a master's degree at the University of Nebraska in Lincoln, I was attached to the Air Force ROTC detachment as a student. I had to report to the detachment in uniform once a week and mentored many of the undergraduate ROTC cadets as they prepared to join the Air Force. I was blown away more than 20 years later at my son's high school track meet when one of these ROTC cadets, Mike, now an Air Force colonel, walked up to me and introduced me to his family. He told me he was about to retire and thanked me for being such a good example to follow—I smiled for days after the encounter. Mentoring cadets was not part of my duties at Nebraska but mentoring helps your people and builds your team.

While teaching history at the Air Force Academy, I worked

for Brigadier General Carl Reddel, the History Department Permanent Professor, as his personnel officer. As a personnel officer, I recruited and tracked great Air Force officers to teach in the History Department. Brigadier General Reddel had a unique background, earning a Ph.D. in Russian Studies at the University of Indiana. He told me to find brilliant, passionate officers with unique talents and different perspectives to challenge our cadets and prepare them for the diverse experiences they would live as officers. I had great examples of leaders like this in the department, like Reddel and Colonel Steve Chiabotti, a physics major at the Academy who went on to get his Ph.D. in History from Duke University.

Colonel Chiabotti mentored me to take care of and retain our people by finding the art of the possible in the personnel system and not letting it limit our people. We tried to help our unique people find jobs that captured their passion, knowing that when we did, they would thrive and remain in the Air Force. We often sent our instructors to extraordinary degree programs to fill our mission needs, and we wanted to use and retain their special talents for the Air Force. We worked to help our people do what they loved for the benefit of the Air Force team. Chiabotti taught me how to work with all the different career tribes in the Air Force, both in getting our people to the Academy and placing them after their assignment. Often, the Air Force bureaucracy focused on keeping people on the main path and opposed letting their people teach at the Academy as it took them away from mainstream personnel requirements. By deliberately recruiting, hiring, and outplacing our unique History staff, we tried to find a mutual benefit for both our people and the Air Force. Though we did not always succeed, our people trusted us more for the effort.

REACH OUT TO YOUR TEAM. As a leader, you must reach out to your team members to understand their goals, their concerns, and their own personal development. They won't open themselves to you unless you step out to meet them in their workplace. Your relationship with them should be built on finding mutual benefits to build trust and transparency in the organization. And by the way, I benefitted from our approach at the History Department—my family and I loved our time in Colorado Springs, and I thrived when I stepped back into the mainstream using the skills I learned off the beaten path in the Air Force career that followed.

TAKEAWAYS

Leaders:

- Develop people by understanding their strengths, goals, and family plans to find mutual benefit.
- Fight to build the team the organization needs, even if that means stepping off the beaten path.
- Always follow your instincts when it comes to helping people—be a guide, a mentor, or even just an extra set of listening ears—you never know when their help will resonate.

Figure 1-1: "A C-130 *Hercules* aircraft makes a Low-Altitude Parachute Extraction System (LAPES) supply drop at Jo Ju Air Strip during the joint Korean/U.S. Exercise Team Spirit '89."

Figure 1-2: "Building trust starts with simple relationships like the one between two brothers." The Author with his sons. United States Space Force Guardian and a United States Army Soldier. December 2020

Figure 1-3: Author with a C-130 crew after a mission in Iraq. While a C-130 aircraft commander could order someone on the crew to do something, the best leaders led their crews by example and inspiration. They realized their job revolved around taking care of their people, getting their people the resources they needed, and then ... getting out of the way. August 2007

Figure 1-4: As the base commander at MacDill AFB, the Author visits Tinker Elementary School to read for story time. As a leader, you must reach out to your team members to understand their goals, their concerns, and their own personal development. They won't open themselves to you unless you step out to meet them in their workplace. And sometimes you must step outside your comfort zone to connect with them.

PART 2

H.D. "JAKE" POLUMBO

RETIRED MAJOR GENERAL H.D. "JAKE" POLUMBO is a founding partner of Two Blue Aces, LLC. After 34 years of active service, Major General Polumbo retired in 2015 as commander of the Ninth Air Force in South Carolina, comprising eight active-duty wings in the southeastern United States with more than 400 aircraft and over 29,000 active-duty and civilian personnel. He is also Rob Polumbo's brother.

"Successful leaders and great followers who are on paths to new leadership roles, will immediately understand and appreciate Jake's real-world insights and live-fire experience. While most of us operate at ground level, successful leaders experience opportunities and challenges that often take them to new heights that may have seemed unattainable. In his latest book, Jake spells out the bottom-line skills, attributes, traits, and souls needed to consistently lead others to victories. Using real-world example after example, Jake's experiences are shared with concise and clear detail. Leading warfighters into battles—where coming in first is the only option—is the backdrop for this inspiring and thoughtful leadership synopsis. As leaders of large and small teams, we experience moments of truth each day; and outcomes are determined by how we have prepared for the roles attained. Organizations, companies, athletic teams, and military units depend on successful leaders in order to win. As Jake cites, confident leaders are always refining and enhancing their skills. Great followers often become great leaders because they are willing to learn new skills and apply them, increasing their impact in helping their teams achieve victories. I have spent significant time with many successful leaders—including former Presidents Ford and Carter, Magic Johnson, and CEOs of very successful organizations throughout the United States. Each of these prominent individuals embodies the winning persona and passion for what it takes to achieve the highest levels of success. Jake's *Leadership at 100 Feet* will have you and your teams flying at MACH SPEED to new heights!"

John Cassidy

CEO (Ret), Sierra Central Credit Union,
Yuba City, California

CHAPTER 6

PERSEVERANCE, DETERMINATION, AND SHEER DOGGEDNESS

> "Have a bias towards action—let's see something happen now. You can break that big plan into small steps and take the first step right away."
> —Indira Gandhi

I STARTED MY CAREER in the United States Air Force with a leadership and marketing challenge that turned out pretty successful—if I say so myself. My name is Harry D. Polumbo, Jr., also known as "Jake." How I got that nickname is a life lesson in itself—one of perseverance, determination, and sheer doggedness.

I grew up in the citrus-growing and water-skiing town of Winter Haven, Florida, and my family and high school friends—including my good friend Todd Dantzler—called me by my given middle name—Dennis. This name stayed with me during my four years at the US Air Force Academy in the late '70s, continuing into my early years in the Air Force through 1982 when I transitioned into flying the Lockheed Martin F-16 Fighting Falcon, aka the "Viper." And that's when, during my first assignment at Nellis Air Force Base in Nevada, my marketing campaign began. Early in my tour at Nellis, I learned all new fighter pilots were assigned "callsigns"—or nicknames—that likely stuck with them the rest of their careers. Since my initial callsign was not very impressive and actually kind of degrading, I decided to get rid of it at any cost!

Thus, my marketing campaign was born. My quest for a new callsign began small. I asked my close friends to start calling me "Jake" when we were flying—a name I had suggested for my first-born son but got overridden by my high school sweetheart and now wife, Sandra. I put this new, personally selected, callsign on all my coffee mugs, helmet bags, and Friday night nametags, hoping for the best! This was branding at the grassroots level. Selecting your own callsign in a fighter squadron, it turns out, was frowned upon by the elder statesmen in the community, but after another year or two of persistence, tenacity, and a lot more cash, I became known as "Jake" to all my friends and even, reluctantly, to my superiors who still remembered my original rotten callsign. To this day, most of my colleagues from the Air Force still think my given name in life is "Jake" Polumbo. Mission complete!

After my first operational assignment in the 428 Tactical Fighter Squadron, aka the "Buccaneers," I went on to command at the squadron, group, and three times at the wing level in the '90s and 2000s. Air Force squadrons usually have 300 or more people in them, groups can be as large as 1,000 people, and wings—or bases—often include three-to-five thousand workers and nearly three times more family members and dependents who call that base their home. Later in my career, in 2012, I had the distinction of commanding a task force of 5,000 men and women in Afghanistan, followed by command of the storied Ninth Air Force headquartered at Shaw Air Force Base in South Carolina from 2013 to 2015. There were almost 30,000 workers assigned under my command, and each of those workers had family members who needed their leader—really all the leaders in the command—to do their jobs with integrity and honesty, 24/7, and keep their loved ones safe during combat and training missions around the world. My growth as a leader in the Air Force was gradual, and I had to work on it each time the challenges increased in a new position where I would lead even more people. The Department of Defense and Air Force value leadership development and invest heavily in it. The effectiveness of leadership is tested out in life-or-death situations in the field where the stakes are at their highest. The following pages draw from my considerable experience in the military with applications for civilian situations.

Throughout this story, I'll try to convey how I learned to be a more effective and compassionate leader each day since so many people counted on me to help keep their lives in proper balance.

In effect, these lessons, learned over the course of my 34-year military career, continually refined my leadership skills so I wouldn't ultimately "flame out" in my next job.

NEAR ROCKS, FAR ROCKS. During my first three assignments in the Air Force, I was categorized as a Company Grade Officer (CGO) who needed to learn how to fly, fight and win as one small part of a much larger fighter squadron. My leaders, mentors, and instructors in these squadrons were more experienced fighter pilots in the F-16 than I was, so they were usually "on point" of the two-and four-ship formations I flew in daily during the 1980s. Each morning, our team briefing included a simple adage for the junior members in the formation to operate under, a quote that stuck with me even today in my civilian career. As our formations regularly flew at a couple of hundred feet above the terrain at speeds approaching 600 miles per hour, our flight leaders told us to carefully follow this cadence: regularly check on the near rocks, then scan the far rocks, followed by a careful look at your leader's jet, and finally turn around and "check six" for enemy aircraft that might have snuck up on us! A lot is wrapped up in that simple, catchy phrase. Let me explain.

As a follower—or wingman—on these early missions in my career, I needed to make sure my airplane never impacted the ground in front of me, and that task required a lot of concentration early in my flying career, especially at high speeds. Once I was sure I could stay above the terrain for the next 30 seconds or so, I then tried to think ahead about important tasks coming up—like fuel checks, navigation updates, radio calls, and ultimately, things I would need to do in the target area, like dropping a bomb on the correct target or avoiding missiles and guns protecting the target. In each check of both the near rocks and the distant mountains, I also needed to keep an eye on my leader to make sure I noticed any signals he might give us to update our course or turn the formation to a new heading due to something he'd seen on his radar or in his scan of the horizon. We didn't always fly the "line" drawn on our maps, so I needed to make sure my leader could change my vector and tasks at any time. This mid-course update is as relevant to today's business world as it was when my fellow pilots and I were trying to navigate to a designated target in enemy territory. Finally, after my frequent checks on the terrain and my leader were accomplished, I was supposed to turn around in the cockpit and look behind me while flying at speeds approaching ten miles a minute. We call this "checking six" in the fighter business—making sure there aren't any bad guys rolling in on our formation that we missed on our radar scopes just minutes before. This wasn't an easy task, but as I gained experience, I got better and better at flying low and fast while looking backward out of the famous bubble canopy of the F-16! This "habit pattern" worked well for F-16s at low altitude and taught me a lot about getting tough missions done in any organization under any circumstances.

Where else does this work? Does this fighter pilot jingle apply to your organization? I think it does. As a worker in a large company, you need to get your own tasks done every day in the prescribed manner so others who are counting on you can get their work done as well. Then, once everyone gets their routine tasks accomplished, the team needs to keep their eyes on the far horizon to ensure the main goal of organizational success—maybe profitability—happens, ensuring the company stays viable well into the future. Workers at all levels of a team should stay attentive to their boss's guidance to make sure adjustments to the company's strategy and plan can be made mid-course. And finally, all people in an organization should be aware of the threats to their business model from outside players and be able to pivot or react swiftly. Prompt reactions are often necessary in a dynamic workspace.

"Near rocks, far rocks, lead, check six" is a short memory jogger to think about when trying to get your job done and be a good teammate in a complex operation. It's also a good way to remind people in your organization that their job matters every day in the office and out in the field. Try it out next week!

TAKEAWAYS

- Make sure to accomplish your routine tasks precisely and completely every day.
- Keep your attention on the team's long-range goals to ensure the company's success.
- Be ready for guidance from your boss, so adjustments to the plan happen quickly.

CHAPTER 7

COMING IN SECOND IS LOSING

"An army of deer led by a lion is more to be feared than an army of lions led by a deer."
—Philip II of Macedon

AS YOU CONSIDER how to train your mid-level supervisors and emerging leaders to do better planning for growth and innovation, I'm reminded of how the United States Military Services trains officers to be problem solvers and, ultimately, leaders in the air, at sea, on the ground, or in space. The US Air Force Weapons School in Nevada is recognized as one of the premier leadership development programs anywhere in the world. My father attended this school in Nevada in the early '50s; I attended the course in 1987 and then became an instructor in the program during the early '90s. Interestingly, my brother Rob attended the demanding course in 1991 when I was an instructor at the school. We were fortunate to fly a couple of missions together during his training, and those stories remain featured topics any time we get together with friends and family.

The six-month leadership course is a graduate-level program for mid-level officers, including academic study and tests, tactics development, planning, and execution, plus a healthy dose of character development with the ultimate expectation of graduating the Air Force's best instructors and future senior leaders. And let me be clear here—the most important goal of the Weapons School in Nevada is to ensure the United States comes in first when military force is used as our primary means of achieving national security goals and objectives. Coming in second during military operations—or maybe even at this stage in your company's existence—is the same as losing. It's probably not a smart goal to adopt a mentality that coming in second is okay, especially in today's competitive economy, so encouraging your people to always strive for their best in any endeavor will often pay dividends to your bottom line each year.

CHANGING YOUR MINDSET. So, how do you and your organization develop this "#1 Is Good" mentality? Let me describe how the Air Force's 'advanced tactics' school runs and how its curriculum includes lessons that might cross over into your organization. The truly unique aspect of the Weapons School is that the Pentagon's human resources department recruits and selects only officers who are very good at what they do to ensure the graduates become the best leaders in the business. The US Navy's Top Gun program is a similarly demanding course in subject matter and training, but the Navy begins with younger aviators than the Air Force, thus graduating more junior-level leaders in the process. Regardless, senior political leaders and military commanders expect some of the nation's toughest battles will be planned and led by aviators who wear the graduate patches of the Air Force Weapons School and the Navy's Top Gun program.

It all starts with classrooms, lessons, and tests. During the academic portion of the Air Force training program, the school's instructors ensure students learn how to critically analyze their team's attributes and operating characteristics under any circumstance by:

- Emphasizing their team's strong points *so they can quickly exploit their competitor's weaknesses.*
- Recognizing their own weaknesses*—or capability gaps—and then taking decisive actions to correct those shortfalls.*
- Discussing opportunities openly with their teammates *and rank-ordering the ones that will really make a difference.*
- And finally, honestly assessing the factors and threats *that could lead to mission failure and then eliminating them.*

Sound familiar? These analytics look a lot like the common Strengths, Weaknesses, Opportunities, and Threats*—or SWOT*—analysis utilized in businesses all over the world today.

NEXT IS APPLICATION. Using this framework for analysis, tactical leaders in the Weapons School, and business leaders in your organization, can apply what they've learned in the classroom to real-life situations. Once planning for a mission is complete, the students transition to the demanding flying training portion of the program and are taught to execute each plan precisely, making immediate assessments while flying to see if things are working properly. If they are—the leaders are trained to stick with the plan no matter how confusing the airborne battle gets. If their plans are not working, they are encouraged to dissect the problems quickly, communicate with others succinctly, and adjust "on the fly." If the results are poor due to human errors, these pilots quickly determine during the debrief why their own mistakes happened and then adjust during their next try at the same mission.

Often, these leaders-in-training discover that the actual plan they developed was flawed from the very beginning of the mission. If so, they're taught to admit it without any excuses and implement changes rapidly to avoid dwelling on their own missteps. In today's terms, they're taught to fail quickly, learn from it and do better next time.

This *iterative* process is likely applicable to your business and may lead to better success and profitability. I'm repeatedly reminded that bad news doesn't get better with time, so great leaders need to recognize problems as they develop, embrace them as their own, determine a fix, and quickly put the new plan in motion so their team can succeed. The key to graduating from the

Air Force's Weapons School is the student's honest assessment of his or her team's strengths and weaknesses, stacked against the opportunities they see on the horizon while factoring in the inevitable threats and challenges they're going to encounter.

REJOINING THE TEAM. One final look at the Air Force's six-month curriculum highlights an important "charge" each graduate gets before they go back to the field. This guidance comes directly from the Commandant of the school just before graduation. It is simple but compelling and can be used in your organization when you want experienced leaders to mentor their junior teammates. Once the graduates receive the school's shoulder patch worn on their uniforms, allowing others to recognize their training and expertise, Air Force leaders expect these instructors to be *humble, approachable,* and *credible* toward other members of the organization.

Everyone in the United States military recognize the Weapons School patch and that it sets graduates apart from their peers. However, according to the school's Commandant, this distinction means it is even more important for them to share the knowledge and experiences gained with others who didn't attend this prestigious school. The only way our Air Force remains the best in the world is if each graduate freely shares what they learned with other members of their team so all our nation's Airmen can excel at their job.

And this brings us right back to what I said earlier: in some professions, "coming in second is losing," thus requiring leaders in organizations to be honest with themselves, fair but demanding with their peers and subordinates, and openly willing to share good ideas and techniques with others on their team. Then, and only then, can high-performance teams form up and win in the next competition. It works in the Air Force and can work in your organization too!

TAKEAWAYS

- Ensure your training program teaches people to fail quickly and then move on.
- Encourage your managers to do regular analysis of their operating environment.
- Make sure leaders in your organization are humble, credible, and approachable.

CHAPTER 8

DEVELOPING YOUR LEADERSHIP STYLE

"A leader is a (person) who has the ability to get other people to do what they don't want to do, and like it."
—President Harry S. Truman

DURING MY 34-YEAR military career, I led organizations of varying sizes, from dozens of people all the way to my final position in the historic Ninth Air Force. During my leadership opportunities all over the world, I learned how important it was to be knowledgeable and competent in many areas of the business and to have a dependable, consistent leadership style. Based on feedback from senior people who worked for me during the latter part of my career, my style was open and collaborative, and they appreciated my attempts to keep things relaxed and professional so we could discuss things openly during strategy and planning meetings. During these sessions, I worked hard to develop a consensus among my senior managers but still welcomed differing opinions to avoid "groupthink." However—and this is important—once the time came to decide, I would politely say the discussion was over, make the decision, and give clear guidance so everyone could get on with their own job. Your subordinates will find this leadership quality energizing since it adds efficiency and clarity to your operations. I also recommend writing important guidance down concisely to communicate your decisions to people who aren't in the room for the discussion and ultimate table slap.

But it never really is that simple, is it? One person shouldn't try to make all the decisions in an organization all the time. High-performance teams need a process for delegating authority from a leader to subordinate levels, and this process is a critical component of your leadership style. In each of my leadership opportunities, I encountered varying levels of experience below me in the line of decision-makers and managers. Accordingly, I settled into a simple way of looking at the actual experience level in the company by dividing junior executives into two groups—high-performing, up-and-coming leaders who were ready to conduct independent operations—and the less-experienced managers who needed regular and repetitive coaching to get things done in line with the organization's plan. If I assessed that we had an experienced group of leaders and managers on the team, I was comfortable running collaborative planning sessions, giving broad guidance, and routinely delegating authority to lower levels so that follow-on planning and operations ran efficiently using our people's incredible experience and proven common sense. I also used private mentoring sessions with these gifted leaders to assure them they could count on my support in their decision-making process as long as they avoided the redlines I laid out during strategy sessions. This allowed the first group of leaders to quickly build confidence inside their own operating environment and business operation. If, on the other hand, I assessed my subordinates weren't ready for so much responsibility, I still gave clear guidance during strategy sessions but told them to "get in touch with me first" before taking critical action to prevent any negative impacts to the operation caused by flawed analysis or risky assumptions.

To succeed in today's business world, competent leaders must be confident in their own leadership style and adapt their decision-making process to the experience level of middle managers in their organization. Decisions should be made efficiently at the appropriate level for the good of everyone in the organization, or the company might get beaten by the competition. Your leadership style will be a key component of your company's success; thus, you need to be comfortable with your chosen style. Confident leaders don't waver in their style and are always accountable for the company's overall decisions, regardless of how they got implemented or who made the risky assumptions. Take time early in your career to determine how you will delegate authority since this leadership skill is an important element of high-performance teams and will enable your business and people to thrive. And remember, as a leader, you're always accountable for your own leadership style, as well as your subordinates' actions and decisions ... so choose wisely in these areas.

Good leaders in any organization continually develop and refine their own leadership style and try to become more and more comfortable dealing with chaos and the inevitable changes that occur in almost any business sector today. If you do otherwise, you'll likely be left behind or risk becoming outdated in your own organization.

TAKEAWAYS

- Success is determined by more than one person in a company.
- Groupthink will stifle innovation and minimize creativity in almost any organization.
- Continue to refine your leadership style throughout your career, and always be consistent.

CHAPTER 9

SCHEDULE YOUR PRIORITIES

"Plan for what is difficult while it is easy; do what is great while it is small." —Sun Tzu, *The Art of War*

DURING PROFESSIONAL DEVELOPMENT opportunities early in my career, the Air Force first taught me how to be a good follower before they ever permitted me to be a leader—especially in combat operations. I had to prove to my boss—and to myself—that I could fly high-performance jets at supersonic speeds close to the ground or, even worse, close to the enemy without failing at my tasks and letting other teammates down. Once I could do these things regularly and with confidence, I was designated a leader and had to go through the process of forming my own high-performance teams. This became a demanding scenario since I quickly found myself married and raising two young sons, all of whom wanted some of my time and attention each day and night. The more I moved up the chain of command in the Air Force, the more demands were made on my time—including weekends, evenings, and holidays. And when the leadership positions I found myself in required extensive travel and preparations, I realized I needed a much better way of controlling my schedule as a leader, a husband, and a father. I also came to realize that I was often missing valuable recharge time, the time I needed for myself to read, exercise, and play an occasional round of golf.

As a squadron commander in charge of hundreds of people at Osan Airbase in South Korea, I quickly ran into the age-old problem of not having enough hours in the day. My operation had workplaces all over the base and detachments around the country, so my span of control was wide since, literally, I seemed to have people working everywhere. My boss, at the time, was a true leader himself and very supportive of his subordinate leaders. We all enjoyed working for him since he was a gifted, hands-on fighter pilot and commander. I was still flying the F-16 as an instructor pilot in the 36th Fighter Squadron, nicknamed the "Fabulous Flying Fiends," and we were always ready to go across the border into North Korea on the first night of a war that could begin at any time. We knew these first few missions across the border would be flown in high-threat conditions and through all kinds of rotten weather. So my days at Osan regularly rolled into the night, and I ultimately had to modify my complaint of this unique scheduling challenge into: "There aren't enough hours in my day *or* my night!"

A FAMILY BUSINESS. My success leading this large and diverse unit during the late '90s depended upon my ability to put the most important things on my schedule in the correct order of priority while still maintaining some balance in my own personal life. This was not an easy task during the hyperactive days on the Korean peninsula in the late '90s. Kim Jong Il was the cantankerous leader of the regime in North Korea during those years, and he did not like having the United States military in his backyard. Interestingly my father fought in the Korean War in the early '50s and flew P-80 *Shooting Stars* with the Fiends, logging over 100 combat missions in the last year of the war. I was very proud to maintain his legacy of service and courage along with my brother, who also "stood the watch" on the Korean Peninsula in the 80th Fighter Squadron during the late '80s. The U.S. military have always been a family-oriented business. Sons and daughters of service members (called "brats") see how important their parent's service was to their development as a leader and often follow their veteran mother or father into the business. Often military service becomes a birthright—or a privilege—that is something to be proud of in any family that encourages service to a higher cause.

In later command positions, I definitely learned how to refine my scheduling techniques to ensure I maintained a better balance in my busy professional and personal lives. During these leadership opportunities, I coined the phrase "schedule your priorities, and don't let other people reprioritize your schedule..."

to help me stay focused on the important things in my daily and weekly routine. Only after a particularly challenging command opportunity in the United Arab Emirates did I add another caveat to the end of my quote: " … unless it's your boss!" During my time in UAE, at a base called Al Dhafra, our team was flying combat missions across Iraq, Afghanistan, and even over "The Horn of Africa" every day and night—365 days a year. We had to "*schedule our priorities*" every day, or our fellow warfighters around the Middle East might miss some part of the war plan that could jeopardize the battle they were engaged in or, worse, cost lives. My boss was headquartered at Al Udeid Airbase in Qatar, and he could change our schedule at any time with a simple phone call to me or my deputy. It was paramount that we knew how to adjust "on the fly" in our complex operations, and I encouraged my subordinates to embrace these short-notice changes to our operations when orders came from the top. Instead of grumbling about the disruption to their daily routine based on high-level inputs, our team learned how to be agile in execution, which resulted in a can-do attitude and a "high-performance" label for our team.

Things settled down in my life after those two assignments, but I continued to use this catchy quote to help my subordinates understand how we needed to plan our time better each day to match the needs of the broader team's operating conditions.

SCHEDULE YOUR PRIORITIES. Most leaders seem to have a lot to do every day. However, not all events on their calendar are really *that*

important, so rookie leaders often find it simpler to put easy things on their schedule first before trying to find the proper amount of time to do the tougher tasks necessary to ensure success. To guard against this pattern of *easy* scheduling, especially in big organizations, I would often sit in my home or the office on a quiet weekend with full control of my calendar app. Then, I'd consider the most important tasks I had to do in the next couple of months, such as promotion boards, salary negotiations, hiring and firing decisions, and strategy sessions. Those events would go on my schedule first with a good buffer on the front and back ends of the meeting dates to ensure my travel plans were not train wrecks waiting to happen. Then, I'd put other important dates and events on my calendar like anniversaries, family vacations, and outings with my friends that I truly wanted to be a part of, even though I knew some of them would be overcome by work priorities at some point down the road. Today, I'm more certain than ever that if you fail to put vacations, enjoyable outings, or even coaching your child's team on the calendar well in advance, it's likely that somebody—your secretary or executive assistant—will fill in those white spaces quickly without even thinking of your personal life. If something is important enough for you to look forward to, you need to be wise enough to put it on your calendar as a priority right away and *then* see if it survives first contact with your boss's expectations or simply other important taskings that pop up.

OPEN OFFICE HOURS. My next suggestion is important even though it might defy another important anecdote of good leadership championed by other reputable authors. My thought is to be careful when telling your subordinates that you have an open-door policy since you may be conditioning them to assume it's okay to interrupt you at any time of the day, regardless of the work or task that's already on *your* calendar. If the people who work for you need regularly scheduled time with you, they should plan it appropriately by asking your assistant to put it on the calendar each week in a predictable way—maybe even during your designated "open office" hours. Otherwise, what you're trying to do on, say, a Friday afternoon before heading home for the weekend can often be over-ridden by a subordinate who hasn't done a good job prioritizing his or her schedule and waits until the last minute to decide on an important issue for their part of the operation. If you permit this type of behavior from managers in your company, you are training your people to seek your guidance whenever it's convenient for them and not necessarily when you have the time available for those types of discussions. This is a finer point of *"Schedule your priorities ... "* but one that needs to be understood by you and your executive assistant well in advance of those time-critical decisions you need to make in a quiet conference room or even in your home office.

And one more reminder, again, that everyone likely has a boss and needs to be flexible regarding their calendar. The good news over my career is that most of my bosses already practiced this time-honored skill of "scheduling their own priorities" and not just letting other people reprioritize their busy schedules. An experienced CEO respects their subordinates' time and prioritization efforts and rarely interrupts someone in a key leadership position without a very good reason.

SMART EMAIL. Another important aspect of your time-management skills is managing your information processing and, ultimately, your decision-making process using electronic mail. Many books and articles have been written about how to manage hundreds of emails each day, and a broad summary probably says simply that good leaders need to structure their day by knowing when to do email and when not to. If all you do each hour of every workday is respond to dozens of messages and texts from your subordinates and superiors alike, you'll let electronic mail prioritize your daily work schedule. Instead of this popular, but ineffective technique—doing email all day long and well into the night—plan your days around when you actually *need* timely information to make decisions, and then teach your employees how to send you timely, short, well-written messages providing sufficient background on the subject, plus a desired suspense. And if they need guidance, they should be very clear in the final portion of the note asking you for help.

In 2012, when I was the Chief of Staff of US Africa Command in Stuttgart, Germany, I asked people who worked for me to write "*Info*" or "*Action*" on the subject line before the title so I knew whether they just wanted to let me know something from the message ... i.e., info, or they actually wanted me to do something very important ... i.e., action was required! If the message was info-only, I would open it by the end of the day and prioritize my response for the next day, depending on the importance of the information. My teammates knew they wouldn't likely get a response from me on "*Info*" emails until the next day. But for those important messages where the managers put "*Action*" in the subject line, I would try to open the message as soon as possible. If they were correct in their assessment, I'd usually write a quick note back saying I was "on it" and then take care of it as soon as I could during the remainder of my day, sometimes with a short phone call to discuss things in a little more detail. However, if my people were attempting to reprioritize my schedule due to their tardiness on an important issue—or were working on a routine matter—I would call them, offer a quick bit of guidance, and then suggest they prioritize their own schedule a little better and not always use my time to get caught up.

Email and text messages are important tools in any organization, but workers can abuse them at all levels. Leaders should develop electronic mail protocols for all, including themselves. Sending people messages at all hours of the day and night, and on weekends, tends to develop bad habits across the workforce and ultimately degrades morale in the organization, not to mention the team's overall effectiveness. Good leaders recognize the importance of these leadership techniques and usually mentor their subordinates to do the same. Try these timely tools out soon to keep priorities on your schedule, and then see what you think!

TAKEAWAYS

- Put the most important events on your calendar first and deal with the rest later.
- Ensure people on your team seek your guidance at an appropriate time for you.
- Use electronic messaging smartly in your organization and train others to do the same.

CHAPTER 10

DEVELOPING NEW LEADERS IN YOUR ORGANIZATION

> "If your actions create a legacy that inspires others to dream more, learn more, do more and become more, then, you are an excellent leader." —Dolly Parton

---

IN MY FINAL LEADERSHIP POSITION in the Air Force from 2013 until 2015, I was in charge of five large installations across the southeastern United States, and various smaller units spread out from Texas to Montana. Traveling to these bases and places from our Ninth Air Force Headquarters in South Carolina presented challenges on my calendar and in how I "scheduled my priorities." The team included nearly 30,000 Airmen and civilians in the command and counted over 450 combat- and training-coded aircraft necessary for military operations around the world. Ninth Air Force personnel were as diverse in their skills as I ever could have imagined, from engineers and carpenters in rapidly deployable construction units to high-performance jet fighter pilots, to doctors, nurses, and administrators at our clinics and hospitals on the bigger bases. When I took command of Ninth Air Force, I knew instinctively that my most important job in this new position would be to develop and select future leaders for these organizations to ensure our high-performance teams accomplished tough missions assigned by our nation's leaders in the Pentagon or by our combat commanders out in the field. This would be the biggest leadership challenge of my career, and I set out systematically to build diversity of thought and uniqueness of experience in the command, from the top down and the bottom up.

One of the things I did during my first trip around the command with my new management team was to look around the table during those early meetings to see if or why everyone looked and sounded just like me. I discovered they often did, persuading me to review our leader development programs in Ninth Air Force to ensure fairness and open-mindedness prevailed, hopefully resulting in the best leaders getting promoted to higher levels of responsibility. From my experience through the years, this HR review would result in a broader perspective and wider viewpoint for our management team in all our operations. I didn't do this because senior leaders in the Pentagon told me to do so; I did it because it was the right thing to do in an organization requiring high-performance teams. The challenge for any leader, not just me, was to do the review in a way that made the organization better, not just "more diverse." Given this discussion and my conclusions, let me run through some ideas you should consider in your own organization.

AVOID GROUPTHINK. During all my encounters with the professionals of Ninth Air Force, I wanted to avoid "groupthink" at all costs, especially during strategy meetings and our operational planning sessions. The best way to lose a battle or an important competition is to tell your managers and subordinates what you're thinking at the beginning of a deliberation because you might find out everyone routinely agrees with you without challenging your facts and assumptions.

During the next few months in command, I realized I needed to be more proactive in refining our leadership development programs to ensure we concentrated on the most important aspects of good leadership, not simply enabling popularity contests. In our earlier book, *Leadership From 30,000 Feet*, my colleagues and I outlined the five attributes of great leaders: competence, commitment, courage, compassion, and character. I wholeheartedly preached these "5Cs" to my subordinates in Ninth Air Force during base and organizational visits. From my perspective, leaders in the command needed to be fully competent at what they were trained to do, had to be 100% committed to the mission, and, in particular, needed to care about their people's well-being and development. These "must dos" meant that leaders possessed both the moral courage of their convictions as well as the confidence and tenacity to stand up against improper orders from bad leaders in the military (yes, we have them, too). Mastering these first three attributes of good leadership was the baseline requirement for being considered for higher levels of responsibility in Ninth Air Force. The last two characteristics I emphasized during my mentoring sessions—compassion for fellow workers and character and integrity in all dealings—became essential requirements for anyone who hoped to be competitive for promotion to the senior levels in the organization. Once I outlined these five characteristics of good leadership for my subordinate commanders to consider during officer and non-commissioned officer evaluations, I required them to follow the list carefully when making recommendations to me for promotion to a higher rank and ultimately placing those women and men in key leadership positions inside our squadrons. Remembering again that Ninth Air Force spread across the United States, I had to develop and enforce this "standardization process" to adequately compare and contrast personnel from across the command. Doing so allowed me to perform my job efficiently and fairly, especially when I didn't personally know everyone in the organization.

From this point in my overall assessment of our leadership development programs, I realized my own assessment process needed a careful review and required constant improvement to make sure I didn't permit—knowingly or unknowingly—any bias in the rating process. I took a thoughtful look at my own inclinations toward certain types of people and specific qualifications and training. Since I was in command of Ninth Air Force for more than two years, I decided to keep statistics on all the ratings and assessments we did in the command to ensure we were transparent in our processes and could filter out unwanted biases early, and at any point, in the cycle. This wasn't an easy task, but it proved valuable over my tenure, and I feel confident my successors found the data useful. For leaders of big organizations, if you find that HR analytics and metrics are lacking when you take over your new position, immediately begin the process of developing new and refined metrics, including accurate tracking systems so you can assess how fair your promotion process is after only a few rating cycles. Don't wait ... since it's too important to your business's overall health and success and will result in a culture of accountability across the organization. Your subordinates will appreciate the transparent way you run the company and ultimately select new leaders for your high-performance teams. You'll discover quickly that people who truly want to be the best and get the next promotion will embrace this process and likely become the leader who manages a high-performing team under difficult circumstances. Arrange your promotion system and leader development programs in a way that benefits the team first and not necessarily the people who've been in the company the longest.

I also knew instinctively I needed to plan ahead in Ninth Air Force to drive more diversity of thought into the organization while still rewarding hard-working people with long-standing tenure. This meant I had to talk with my subordinate leaders well in advance of their rack-and-stack assessments so I could identify what we needed in, say, the engineering corps, the logistics department, the pilot ranks, or whatever specialty we were seeking new leaders in at the time. It wasn't always obvious to the managers of my units what "type" leader the Air Force needed for future operations, so we would regularly and consistently talk things over to ensure they mentored their own managers in the best way possible. This guidance meant, for example, that doctors needed to search for and accomplish specialized training necessary for deployed and austere medical operations in Iraq or Afghanistan or that pilots needed to complete specific leader development courses before they would be considered for squadron command. Planning and preparation were as important to the young lieutenants in the organization as they were at the command's most senior officer level.

But how could I increase diversity of thought in squadrons that didn't always reflect the societal and cultural diversity of the general population in the United States? And to make things even more challenging, I knew our squadron commanders needed to evaluate who they had in their organization at that point in time and not necessarily hope for some specific mix of people and experience far into the future. The situation required more thoughtful analysis than just concluding our current processes favored one type of leader over another. So, I continued to review and refine our selection process in the command since I wholeheartedly believed that various leaders and leadership styles in an organization make the whole team stronger in the long run.

Another thing I tried to do in Ninth Air Force was to collaborate more regularly with other commanders at my level in order to try and build a more diverse team. Sometimes, the very person we needed in a squadron in, say, Georgia was actually stationed at a colleague's base in Virginia, and that individual was more than willing to relocate to get the new position. All it took was a phone call or two to make the transfer happen, and suddenly, one commander's "spare" logistician was another squadron's gain. As you would imagine, this required additional long-range planning efforts, but the results were always worthwhile, and our high-performance teams inevitably reflected the new variety of thought at all leadership levels in Ninth Air Force. I would also search for trusted experts outside the Air Force with different experiences than my own, especially when they impressed me with their judgment, creativity, and overall perspective. I often asked them to visit our squadrons at a base and assess the diversity of thought and willingness to listen from within the commander's staff. I was most interested in the staff's willingness to consider new ideas and procedures in order to stimulate innovation and change. And when we really liked these experts after a visit, we always tried to establish more permanent relationships so multiple teams could benefit from their experience. It's exciting to think of all the innovative HR techniques and programs available in the workplace today to develop leaders who form effective, high-performance teams and improve the overall success and profitability of your organization!

A LEADER'S MOST IMPORTANT JOB. Spending quality time and focusing your effort on the organization's leader development programs will make a huge impact on your team's performance and ultimately keep the company successful and make it more profitable. Mentoring junior leaders on their evolving leadership style and decision-making skills will pay big dividends when you select them to head up important projects. Investing in your people and their skills early in their careers will permit you to step back at some point and let others lead and make significant decisions. If you do these essential HR functions now as the leader of your organization, you'll find that selecting and promoting future leaders becomes easier and easier, thus ensuring the overall success of your company in the ever-changing markets of tomorrow.

Good luck!

TAKEAWAYS

- Review your leader development programs often to remove any biases in your selection process.
- Ask outside experts to assess the diversity of experience in your company to build better teams.
- Be generous with your time and talk to your people about your own leadership story!

Figure 2-1: The Author presides over the retirement ceremony of Ninth Air Force Command Chief Master Sergeant Scott Fuller, Shaw Air Force Base, South Carolina, 2015

Figure 2-2: The Author presents a medal to a French Army Soldier, Kandahar Air Base, southern Afghanistan, 2012

Figure 2-3: The Author thanks a friend at his 50th Birthday celebration following a successful Operation Iraqi Freedom U-2 mission, Al Dhafra Air Base, UAE, 2009

Figure 2-4: The Author presents a commander's coin to a US Army Soldier, Jalalabad, eastern Afghanistan, 2013

PART 3

CHAD FRANKS

RETIRED MAJOR GENERAL CHAD “SPARKY” FRANKS is a senior consultant with Two Blue Aces, LLC. After 31 years of service, General Franks retired as the commander of 15th Air Force in South Carolina. He was responsible for over 13 wings, 800 aircraft and over 47,000 Airmen.

"This manuscript is a clear illustration and window into the mind of how effective and successful leaders think about their mission and those under their charge. The tenets captured in these writings can be used not only by warrior leaders but also by leaders raising a family, those in a Fortune 500 company, and everyone in between. General Franks identifies the qualitative behaviors of leaders in every successful command culture. The tangible takeaways provided here should be studied and modeled by every leader who directs humans in complex, ambiguous environments."

Bob Doyle

Current global business leader
Former Recon Marine, USMC
Los Angeles Deputy Fire Chief (Ret)

CHAPTER 11

SIGNIFICANCE VS. SUCCESS

"Coaching gives one a chance to be successful as well as significant. The difference between those two is that when you die your success comes to an end. When you are significant, you continue to help others be successful long after you are gone. Significance lasts many lifetimes."
—Coach Lou Holtz

I WAS BORN and raised in south Louisiana, where I enjoyed hunting, fishing, and all outdoor activities in general. I grew up on crawfish, gumbo, jambalaya, red beans and rice, and all the great Cajun dishes of the South. I enjoyed participating in and watching sports—the team concept and the challenges of the competition are what drew me in. And my dad loved sports (Geaux Tigers! Go Saints!) which gave us something we could always do together.

From an early age, I wanted to join the military because many in my family had served, including my dad, as a communication soldier in the US Army. He was the first leader I had the ability to watch day-to-day run his organization and lead his people. And those early observations of someone who was very good at it formed a foundation that led me to believe that leadership is learned. I took what I learned from those observations and that foundation to pursue a military commission.

I joined the Air Force in 1990 after graduating from the University of New Orleans Air Force ROTC program. I was fortunate enough to spend over 31 years doing what I love more than anything—flying and leading people. I started my career as an air traffic control officer, where I learned the procedures for flying and had the opportunity as a young officer to lead the Air Force's incredible enlisted corps.

I eventually ended up attending Undergraduate Pilot Training (UPT) and chose to fly helicopters, a non-standard path in our Air Force. My first flying assignment was at the 55th Special Operations Squadron at Hurlburt Field, Florida. I flew special operations missions for four years and observed and participated with elite high-performing teams across our military services. It served as the foundation for how I would approach our flying mission, leadership, and developing similar high-performing teams for the rest of my time in the Air Force. I went on to fly as an instructor for our UPT course, a great experience teaching and coaching young officers. After a year of Professional Military Education (PME) at Maxwell Air Force Base, Alabama, and a short staff tour at Special Operations Command at MacDill Air Force Base, Florida. I had the opportunity to serve in several leadership positions within the Combat Search and Rescue helicopter community. I was privileged to command the 66th Rescue Squadron at Nellis Air Force Base in Las Vegas, Nevada, which was one of the best assignments for me since, in the Air Force, we go to war at the squadron level. I was fortunate enough to take my squadron to combat on two occasions, watch them do incredible things, and, most importantly, we were able to bring everyone home.

I went on to command the Rescue Group at Moody Air Force Base, Georgia, which consisted of the Rescue triad of HH-60Gs, HC-130s, and our pararescue squadrons. Following that command tour, I was selected as the first helicopter pilot to serve as the Chief of Staff in our Middle East Air Operations Center for the Combined Forces Air Component Commander. This center is where we executed air operations for the Afghanistan and Iraq conflicts. It was a very busy year, but one filled with many leadership learning opportunities. I went back to Moody as wing commander, following the yearlong deployment, where I was responsible for 5,500 Airmen consisting of six groups and 31 squadrons and comprised of 105 aircraft and $1 billion in assets across four states. A wing commander, much like a CEO, has an enormous impact on the mission and the lives of their people, in my case, our Airmen. It was one of the highlights of my career, but I didn't realize how many more opportunities lie ahead.

The next significant assignments came as I entered the general officer ranks. First was a tour in Air Force Space Command as the 14th Air Force vice commander. This fascinating job took me completely out of my comfort zone into a mission set I knew little about. Because of my experience in special operations and my helicopter background, I provided a different perspective to the space community. The second opportunity came for me with another one-year deployment to Iraq as the deputy commanding general for operations and intelligence for Operation Inherent Resolve—a very challenging mission set with a very diverse force. The operation had 77 participating nations and all U.S. military services involved in destroying the ISIS caliphate and also tasked with rebuilding the Iraqi military. There were many unique challenges trying to form a team among such a diverse force. Finally, I finished my military career as the first helicopter pilot to lead the largest numbered Air Force, the Air Combat Command 15th Air Force. As commander of over 47,000 Airmen and 800 aircraft, I thoroughly enjoyed mentoring and motivating our wing commanders as they worked through the challenges of high operations tempo, racial tensions, and a global pandemic. It was a challenging but very rewarding final command in my military service.

Today, many of those wing commanders would ask me how do you define success. Obviously, there is a myriad of right answers as to what makes a leader successful. It could be meeting objectives, goals, metrics, market share, profit, or mission accomplishments. But the real question is what is more important ... being successful or being significant? Coach Lou Holtz once stated, "Coaching gives one a chance to be successful as well as significant. The difference between those two is that when you die, your success comes to an end. When you are significant, you continue to help others be successful long after you are gone. Significance lasts many lifetimes. That is why people teach, why people lead, and why people coach." When you are significant in the lives of those you lead, your success will go with them and remain long after you move on ... this is the goal ALL leaders should strive to accomplish. So, my answer was always to define your success on how significant you are to those you lead, i.e., having a large and important influence on others.

And, in order to be significant to those you lead, you just have to have **CARE**—be a **C**ommunicator, be **A**ctive, be **R**espectful and be **E**ncouraging! All of us military types LOVE our acronyms, but this one is particularly significant for you as you lead your people.

- Be a **Communicator** with those you lead. Tell them what you believe and the values that are important to you. Talk with them about your successes, but, more importantly, don't be afraid to share your failures with them. Communication requires you to listen ... listen to what is important in their careers and lives. Listen to their personal stories and understand how their personal lives are going.

- Be an **Active** leader. Get out! Get out of the office or from behind your desk. Interact with your people and show you are approachable. Engage them where they work. People don't care who you are; they want you to know who ***they*** are. Use every opportunity that presents itself to engage with your followers—like walking down the hall to a meeting, grabbing a cup of coffee in the break room, visiting with airmen on breaks at conferences, or looking for any opportunities that present themselves outside of work in a social setting. These are all ways to get to know and understand those you lead on a personal level. These opportunities are invaluable, not only to you but to them as well.
- Be **Respectful** of all your followers. Respect their cultures, their differences of opinion, their different experiences, their different attitudes, and their different viewpoints. Every one of your followers has had a different journey in life to get where they are in the organization. Some may have had very fortunate opportunities with a great family life, attending elite schools, and stable finances growing up. But some may have had extremely tough hardships and challenges, both personal and professional, that they had to overcome to get to the same place. Each one deserves respect due him or her.

- Be an **Encouraging** leader. Show your people how much you enjoy being part of their team, how much you enjoy what the organization is getting done, and the problems they are solving. Smile, laugh, and be enthusiastic about what you do. A leader's job is to encourage everyone on the team to reach their full potential!

In early 2021 my dad passed away just seven months prior to my retirement from the Air Force. His passing cemented what I had always believed about leading people ... that being significant to others is more impactful than just worrying about your own success. I realized that even after my dad was gone, he continued to help me and so many others continue to be successful ... and ***that*** is what being significant is all about.

TAKEAWAYS

- Strive to be significant to those you lead.
- To be significant, you have to CARE ... be a Communicator, be Active, be Respectful, and be Encouraging.
- Being significant will ensure your success long after you are gone.

CHAPTER 12

GOOD TO BETTER

"Champions aren't champions because they do extraordinary things, they are champions because they do the ordinary things better than anyone else."
—Chuck Noll

FROM 2012 TO 2013, I was deployed to Al Udeid Air Base in Qatar, serving as the Chief of Staff for US Air Forces Central Command and the Combined Forces Air Component Commander (CFACC), Lt Gen Dave Goldfein, who would later go on to be Chief of Staff of the Air Force. The Combined Air Operations Center (CAOC) is a central location that integrates and synchronizes airpower at the operational level of war.

Through its five divisions, Strategy (SRD); Combat Plans (CPD); Combat Operations (COD); Air Mobility (AMD); and Intelligence, Surveillance, and Reconnaissance (ISRD), each comprised of joint and coalition experts, the CAOC translates strategic decisions to tactical level execution. It was a long and challenging year but very rewarding from a leadership perspective.

From the CAOC, we ran the air wars for both Iraq and Afghanistan with a team of some of the best colonels in the Air Force. While having so much talent in one organization was great, it was also challenging to mold that much talent into a cohesive team. The good news was that I had a front-row seat to watch Lt Gen Goldfein take all that talent and do tremendous work for the air campaign. At the time, I also didn't know that front-row seat would pay off in my next assignment. While at Al Udeid, I was eligible to compete on the wing command list. The Air Force runs an annual board to select colonels who will be wing commanders. I was very honored to find out I would return to the base I deployed from and take command of the 23rd Wing, Flying Tigers. The 23rd Wing is one of the largest wings in Air Combat Command, with over 5,500 Airmen spread across four states. Their main mission was Close Air Support, executed with the A-10 Warthog and Combat Search and Rescue by the HH-60 Pave Hawk, HC-130 Combat King and Guardian Angel weapons system. I had just finished my group command at Moody Air Force Base in Georgia prior to deploying to Al Udeid, and I was very excited about the opportunity to command at the wing level—until I realized the daunting challenge I would have to face.

After spending two years at Moody as the 347th Rescue Group Commander before deploying, I knew the 23rd Wing was a high-functioning and excellent organization. The wing had executed its mission flawlessly and was known across Air Combat Command as one of its top combat wings. Not only that, but my good friend, whom I had known since my special operations days, was the sitting wing commander. We spent our squadron command and group command tours together. We served in combat together, and he was a popular and well-known warrior within the Rescue community. Taking over an organization already performing well from an outstanding leader who has done exceptional work was a daunting challenge I knew I would be facing.

EXPECTATIONS. I was excited on the day of the change of command. It was a beautiful day in south Georgia, and the wing did a great job getting the ceremony set up. Everyone was extremely helpful with the transition to ensure I got off to a good start; however, I could still see the apprehension in everyone's eyes about the new guy. I could feel the concern about the wing taking a downturn from their progress under the outgoing commander. After all, every new commander comes in and changes things, right? Well, that might be true with a new leader coming into an organization that is performing poorly or has a bad work climate, but in this case, the wing had neither of those issues, so I had to develop a strategy to take this well-performing wing and make it better.

IDENTITY. The first thing I did following the change of command was sit down with the senior leaders, my group commanders, and group chief master sergeants to give them my expectations. This was a technique I used in every organization I commanded. People want to know who is coming in, what makes them tick, and what their expectations are. I gave them a short biography, both professional and personal because they need to know who I am and where I'm from to know where I am going.

TRANSPARENCY. Personal connections are what make every organization cohesive. I gave each of my new command team an already-prepared memorandum laying out what I expected of all leaders at all levels. I also shared that letter with all the Airmen in the wing following the meeting, so they knew what I expected of their leaders—because I believe transparency is necessary to establish an excellent work climate. My initial guidance to them was simple ... nothing changes! They were shocked that the new commander wasn't changing the mission statement or the vision of the organization but also relieved that I wasn't. They all knew they were doing well as an organization, and I wanted us to continue with their already-established success. This initial transparent communication, setting the expectations and providing the initial guidance, was just the beginning of my strategy to get the wing from doing good to doing even better.

INTEGRATION, COMMUNICATION, OBSERVATION. My initial communication with the senior leaders was very important, but getting them to buy into the way ahead would be crucial. I waited about two months before attempting to get buy-in; I wanted to take that time to see what was working well and what may need to be improved. In a well-run organization, the improvements needed may be very small, and on the fringe, if the team is already good at its core mission. To get a good sense of the areas needing improvement, I had to get out and about. I visited all areas of the wing. I went to where the Airmen were working and accomplishing the mission. I talked with the people who got the job done every day. This type of information gathering is very important, as my airmen were not shy about what worked well and what didn't. At this point, observation became an essential part of my strategy before asking the wing to embrace a new direction.

FORWARD MOMENTUM. After this initial observation, it became clear where the wing needed to go and what we needed to do to improve. No matter how good an organization is, it can always find ways to get better. For example, safety issues needed to be addressed; although the mission was getting done, some Airmen noted that shortcuts were being taken. This could not be continued in a flying organization that has lives on the line every day. Another needed improvement arose from the observation of the number of things we required from everyone ... it was starting to overwhelm the Airmen and distract them from our core mission. Now it was time to get the senior leaders in the organization to acknowledge these challenges and find solutions.

BUY-IN. To get the senior leaders to agree on the way forward for the wing, we met off-site for a strategy session. It was critical to get away from the day-to-day business so we could think and discuss without the distractions of everyday tasks. I already knew where I wanted to take the wing, so I was able to guide the discussion and lead them to where I wanted to go while allowing them to bring other ideas to the table. The leader must have a vision but also be flexible enough to be open to diverse thought. What we ended up with was a good strategy to get better and a leadership team that bought into that strategy as their own. Now, all we had to do was get the 5,500 Airmen on board.

BE CLEAR. BE CONCISE. The final piece needed to get the wing moving towards getting even better was the buy-in from those in the organization that do the work daily. Clear and concise communication would be key. Long or wordy mission statements may look good on the wall, but the organization will not embrace or inculcate it. We needed something all could remember and get across the premise of what we were trying to do as a wing. I used an analogy from football ... the Pittsburgh Steelers had won four Super Bowls in just five years and were the best team in the NFL at the time. Someone asked their head coach, Chuck Noll, how he got the team to sustain and even improve after all the success they had. He responded simply by saying: "*Champions aren't champions because they do extraordinary things; they are champions because they do the ordinary things better than anyone else.*" I shortened it to "*Do the Ordinary Things Better Than Anyone Else.*" Although we did have a mission statement for the organization, this short quote became the 23rd Wing "war cry." I posted it everywhere—at the front gate where the Airmen came to work every day, on every slide we used for meetings or all-calls, and I would use the phrase in every address or speech to the Airmen in the wing. It was repetitive, I know, but I wanted it to sink in. I knew this would help address the two main issues we needed to improve ... safety and cutting down on the additional duties that took time away from the core mission.

One day as I spoke at our Airmen Leadership School, Professional Military Education training our Airmen attend prior to becoming a frontline supervisor, I asked the class what made us so good as an Air Force. When one of the students replied, "*because we do the ordinary things better than anyone else,*" I knew we had buy-in! The wing got it, embraced it, and showed they could get even better than they already were ... and they did.

TAKEAWAYS

- Good Leaders always communicate expectations.
- Good Leaders are deliberate about change in an organization.
- Good Leaders always get buy-in from the organization.

CHAPTER 13

DISCIPLINE AND PURPOSE

"Discipline is not what you do to somebody, but what you do for them." —Coach Lou Holtz

---

MY LAST COMMAND in the Air Force was as the 15th Air Force Commander. It comprised 13 Wings and three Direct Reporting Units. Almost half of the wings would change commanders every summer, so I normally did seven-to-eight command changes. Military changes of command follow a long tradition, with each action and wording rooted in a long-standing tradition. As commander, I always gave remarks to begin the ceremony, I would acknowledge the accomplishments of the wing under the outgoing commander, and I would then introduce the incoming commander and highlight his or her background and experiences—identifying attributes that made them the right choice for the job. Then I always told the incoming commander they owed the Airmen two things—Discipline and Purpose! I did this during the ceremony, not just for the commander to hear but for every leader at every level within the organization. My experiences within the Air Force had taught me that discipline and purpose were the two most important things needed to be a high-performance team.

I graduated from Undergraduate Pilot Training (UPT) at Fort Rucker, Alabama, in 1995. I was lucky to have the chance to select an MH-60G as my aircraft and even luckier that it was to Hurlburt Field, Florida, home of Air Force Special Operations Command.

When I arrived at the 55th Special Operations Squadron, I was the first new pilot out of UPT they had seen in years. The squadron was a very experienced group—mostly instructors—and almost all had former HH-60G experience either from Combat Rescue or from the other services. Being a special operations squadron working with the top-tier special operators across the Department of Defense, they were skeptical of the new pilot with zero experience in any aircraft except for training aircraft. My pitch to my new squadron mates was that I was a blank sheet they could help turn into the Air Commando of their choosing. They bought it and embraced me as the little brother they had to show the ropes to and teach the mission of Air Force Special Operations Command. The flying was intense, and the training to get mission-ready was arduous. I learned a lot in the first nine months of being in the squadron, but what surprised me the most was the number one emphasis throughout the squadron—discipline.

DISCIPLINE. Flight discipline was the primary focus for every training sortie and mission. We talked about discipline during planning. We talked about discipline during the preflight briefing. We talked about discipline in the debrief following the flight. We talked about discipline on our training days. It was always about knowing the regulations, the limits of the aircraft, our tactics, techniques, and procedures (TTPs), squadron operating procedures, and squadron standards. It was the foundation of everything we did to get the mission done. People from outside our community often see us as "cowboys" due to the type of flying we would often have to do, such as landing on the wings of an aircraft on the ground or chasing vehicles down the street. Many didn't realize that we were able to do those types of missions because we were disciplined. Knowing where the edges of the boundaries are allows one to make risk-based decisions on whether to go beyond those boundaries in a deliberate manner. This focus on discipline went well beyond the flight line.

Our squadron focused on being disciplined in all aspects of the organization. There was always an emphasis on standards, ensuring we were upholding grooming, uniform, and physical fitness standards. Meetings started on time, and if you were not five minutes early, the door was locked, and you missed the meeting. Every task given to an individual had a completion date and the expectation of meeting it. This may seem very military-like and even extreme, but it served an important purpose.

When a unit is well-disciplined, it tends to perform higher with higher morale among its members. Everyone knows what is expected of them in a well-disciplined organization—there is no guessing about the standard. People are more comfortable and work better with each other when they are all working from the same starting point. Members of a well-disciplined organization tend to be more self-disciplined, which typically leads to more self-control and satisfaction. A disciplined organization is not constricted from being innovative either; it knows where the boundaries are and can better make risk-based decisions on new ways or methods of doing things. In some of the most innovative units I have worked with, many in the special operations community, discipline was at the core of their success. But good organizations need more than just discipline; they also need to ensure everyone within the organization knows their purpose.

HAVE PURPOSE. As a wing commander, there are plenty of demands on your time and attention, some more important than others. Every spring, when the weather is warmer, we open the base pool to the Airmen and their families. The pool manager always had the opening day just for the young Airmen so they could get out and have a social event since many of them were new. They asked me if I would help them with a contest for the Airmen during the pool party, and of course, I went along. They had me go to the pool the day prior so they could time me as I sprinted across the length of the pool in a huge blow-up hamster wheel. I felt ridiculous, but hey, it was for the Airmen. The next day at the pool party, the plan was to have Airmen see if they could beat my time. The prize was my commander's parking spot at different locations around the base for 30 days. I wasn't too excited about that, but again, it was for the Airmen. Airmen lined up to take a shot at the old man, all of whom I believe bested my time. The winner, however, was a young airman basic who worked over at the dental clinic as a dental journeyman. As he came up to claim his prize, I congratulated him on a job well done and informed him he would get rock star parking for the next month. That's when he told me he didn't own a car. At first, I was ecstatic since I wouldn't lose my parking spot, but then I had to quickly figure out a consolation prize for the young Airman. Suddenly it hit me—the perfect solution that truly would make him a rock star. I asked him if I could pick him up and bring him to work in my staff car instead. He went bright-eyed with disbelief and then said, "Absolutely." I told him, "Great, I'll pick you up at 0725, right outside your dorm room." I didn't realize that this gesture and interaction with this young Airman would re-teach me the lesson about purpose.

At 0725, my young Airman looking sharp and ready for work, was standing outside his dorm as I pulled up. After he got in, I said, "Let's go drive around the base a little bit." He became very nervous and told me he could not be late for work. This was very encouraging, and I told him he would be ok and that I knew his boss! We drove to the flight line, and the timing was perfect. Just as we entered, two HH-60 *Pave Hawks* were starting engines to go on a training mission, an HC-130 was taking off down the runway, and four A-10 *Warthogs* were rounding the corner and flashed us a thumbs up from the cockpit. The young Airman couldn't contain himself and said: "Wow, look at that; I didn't know we had A-10s here!" I couldn't believe what I was hearing. When I learned he had been at Moody for nine months, I said: "You have been here nine months and do not know the primary mission of our wing?" Not only that, but he didn't realize that in his job, he made that mission happen. I informed him that those pilots in the cockpit would not be there if not for him signing off on their dental exams, clearing them to fly. He understood immediately and realized his important purpose at the 23rd Wing. I knew then that my leaders across the wing and I had more work to do.

As a leadership team, we needed to ensure that every Airman knew and understood their purpose. I realized that it could not be a one-time thing. Members of an organization can quickly get caught up in the daily grind and forget where they fit in or their purpose. Leaders must continually talk to the members of their teams to ensure they understand and know how important they are to the team. It takes every single member of a unit to make the mission happen!

Discipline and Purpose are the two things that every leader owes their team. Discipline establishes a standard within an organization allowing it to achieve better results than expected. Everyone needs to understand where they fit into the team, their role, and their purpose. When individuals understand their purpose, it encourages them to improve the skills needed to be successful. Discipline and Purpose together are powerful for the team and the individual.

TAKEAWAYS

- A leader owes their followers DISCIPLINE.
- A Leader ensures EVERYONE knows their PURPOSE.
- An organization that is DISCIPLINED and has PURPOSE will be high performing.

CHAPTER 14

LEADERSHIP BOLDFACE

"The strength of the group is in the strength of the leader." —Coach Vince Lombardi

IN 1995 I drove through the gates of Laughlin Air Force Base, where I was to start Undergraduate Pilot Training. It's a year-long training course for Air Force pilots and, from a training perspective, one of the hardest years I had during my 31 years of service. It was intense, pressure-filled days that started early in the morning and usually finished late into the night with studying and preparing for the next day. The days were filled with academics, simulators, or training sorties every day. Our instructors were professional but demanding and ensured that the students were meeting standards. The main area of emphasis from the instructors was aircrew discipline. We were required to know the rules of the air, our aircraft operating limitations, and of course, emergency procedures. There was a weekly test on all of these, and if you didn't pass, you didn't fly until you had a re-test with an instructor. And we only flew in the aircraft once we could demonstrate in a simulator that we knew all the techniques and procedures to safely accomplish the flight.

There were several simulator training rides where we concentrated solely on emergency procedures. We had to be able to analyze the problem quickly, refer to the appropriate checklist, and get the aircraft safely on the ground. In the case of an emergency, we were taught to be methodical and use our checklist to ensure we got it right. We were required to use our checklist in every situation—well, almost every situation!

There are certain emergencies where being able to reference a checklist would not be practical, like an engine fire or the complete loss of an engine. When these types of emergencies are encountered, it requires immediate action from the pilot and knowing the procedures from memory. In the Air Force, we call these emergency procedures, "Boldface." Chapter three of our aircraft technical manuals is always the emergency procedures chapter. It contains all the checklists required for any aircraft emergency. If an emergency and its checklist steps are written in **BOLDFACE**, then it is required to be memorized by the pilot. Pilots are constantly tested on boldfaced procedures. Pilots are required to write them out for their aircraft every month before they are cleared to fly. It is part of their annual checkride as well.

These procedures are so crucial to aircraft operation the pilot must be able to act instantly and instinctually—there is no time to think—and execute the steps as if they are second nature. These boldfaced procedures were a part of my entire Air Force flying career.

As I moved into more and more leadership positions, I began to see there were similar knowledge requirements and duties I must know without referencing a checklist or some leadership book. I began to see the correlation between these boldfaced procedures and leadership. I call them my ***LEADERSHIP BOLDFACE***, and have them committed to memory, reviewed often, so they are always fresh in my mind. Over the years, they have become even more important than my Aircraft ***BOLDFACE*** since they affect the people I lead.

KNOW YOUR JOB/KNOW YOUR PEOPLE. American Revolutionary War General Henry Knox once said: "*Officers can never act with confidence until they are masters of their profession.*" General Knox was correct that you must know your business to lead your team. Your team will be able to tell whether you know what you are talking about or just faking it. A team that does not have confidence in its leader is sure to fail. I would go further than General Knox and say the leader also must know his or her people. What motivates them, their skill levels, family situations at home, goals and career objectives, background, and the experiences that got them to where they are today. This is crucial information for the leader to put the right talent in the right position to be helpful to the team. To be an effective and successful leader, you have to know your area of expertise to have credibility. You have to know your people to make them a team.

SET THE EXAMPLE. General Colin Powell, former Secretary of State and Chair of the Joint Chiefs, said: "*The most important thing I learned is that soldiers watch what their leaders do. You can give them classes and lecture them forever, but it is your personal example they will follow.*" I used to tell commanders that I could visit a unit, walk around talking with its members and tell you what type of leader the commander was. If the team was timid or lacked discipline, so did the commander. If the team was confident and professional, so was the commander. It only takes about six to 12 weeks for an organization to take on the personality of its leader. The members of the organization watch everything the leader does. How they work, how they interact with subordinates, how they interact with superiors, and even how they interact with their peers. They observe how the leader makes decisions and whether they are aggressive or indecisive. The leader sets the tone for the organization's personality through their actions and example.

MAKE DECISIONS. Napoleon Bonaparte stated once, "*Nothing is more difficult, and therefore more precious than to be able to decide.*" A leader's main job is to make decisions. The organization relies upon the leader to take information and make a decision so the team can move forward. Leaders are usually indecisive because they are either risk-averse or require perfect information, paralyzing their organization. There are no risk-free decisions, and there is never perfect information. Leaders may have to make a few more decisions later as the situation or information changes and alter course from the original decision. Still, at least you have the team moving forward. Leaders who are indecisive frustrate the members of their organization. A frustrated organization is a non-productive one. An attitude of non-decision-making from the leader will permeate the organization leading to one incapable of making progress.

DEMONSTRATE COURAGE. General Matthew B. Ridgeway, former Army Chief of Staff, put it this way: "*There are two kinds of courage, physical and moral, and he who would be a true leader must have both.*" In my over 31 years of military service and time served in many combat zones, I have never seen any leader in these intense situations lack the physical courage to lead their units. The American fighting man and woman have demonstrated time and time again physical courage in combat to defend this nation. However, I have seen leaders who lacked the moral courage to do the right thing—having the ability to do what is right all the time, no matter the situation. Having the courage to speak up when perhaps everyone else is going along with the status quo. It is the courage to stand up for what you believe in—even if it means your career will be impacted. It means speaking truth to power even when it may not be popular. Leaders at all levels must have physical courage, but more importantly, they must demonstrate moral courage.

INTEGRITY IS NON-NEGOTIABLE. Air Force General John Ryan, seventh Chief of Staff, said regarding integrity: "*Integrity is the most important responsibility of command. Commanders are dependent on the integrity of those reporting to them in every decision they make. Integrity can be ordered but it can only be achieved by encouragement and example.*" Leaders rely upon the truth in every aspect of decision-making. Integrity is the highest standard that all within the organization must keep. And just as leaders expect integrity from the members of the organization, so to do the members rely on the integrity of the leader. Leaders cannot be effective if their word cannot be trusted. They must set the example of integrity in all aspects—whether in large or small things, or else the erosion of trust will begin. Once a leader has lost the trust of those he or she leads due to a lack of integrity, no matter how slight, they will no longer be an effective leader. To a leader, integrity is everything.

BE LOYAL UP AND DOWN THE CHAIN OF COMMAND. Famous World War II General George S. Patton talked about loyalty this way: "*There is a great deal of talk about loyalty from the bottom to the top. Loyalty from the top down is even more necessary and much less*

prevalent." Often, we see leaders supporting the decisions and actions of those at the top of the organization. It is necessary even when we may not agree to support the decisions of our superiors, but we also need to ensure we are supporting those we lead as well. Too often, we are quick to criticize, discipline, or even end the careers of some whose actions or decisions negatively impact the organization. When an individual fails, we should first look at ourselves before taking quick disciplinary action. Did we give the individual the right training or the proper supervision? Did we set an environment or culture where perhaps members thought it okay to take shortcuts? If so, then it's the leader's job to stand up and take responsibility for the conditions that led to the failure. Being loyal down the chain makes a good leader.

LEADERSHIP BOLDFACE is what we as leaders know and understand without reference to checklists or how-to books. Just like there are different boldface procedures for different aircraft, Leadership Boldface will be different for every individual. Leaders need to take the time to think and reflect on what their Boldface might be.

TAKEAWAYS

- Know your job/know your people.
- Set the example.
- Make decisions.
- Demonstrate courage.
- Integrity is non-negotiable.
- Be loyal up and down the chain.

CHAPTER 15

MENTORING VS. DELIBERATE DEVELOPMENT

> "I would caution you always to remember that an essential qualification of a good leader is the ability to recognize, select, and train junior leaders."
> —General Omar Bradley, US Army

WHEN I ARRIVED at my first flying squadron at Hurlburt Field, Florida, I was excited about learning the special operations mission as quickly as I could. I focused on getting all the appropriate flying qualifications, acquiring as many flying hours as possible to begin upgrading to aircraft commander and flight lead and become an experienced operator. I also had what we termed additional duties in the squadron as well. I began as a scheduler, learning to schedule daily training sorties and prepare personnel for deployments. After that came the role of resource manager for the squadron. (Basically, I became the supply officer ensuring the squadron had everything needed for training, deployments, and mission accomplishment.)

Then I went to the mobility office, responsible for ensuring all personnel and equipment were prepared and ready to deploy to combat at a moment's notice. After only eight months in the mobility office, I was off to our plans shop (responsible for all the squadron planning for exercises, joint training, and operational missions). Every time I got comfortable in a job, the squadron leadership moved me into a different one. I started to believe that perhaps I was not living up to expectations, and they were trying to find something I might be good at! Then one day, my commander told me that I would be the next flight commander in the squadron and explained to me that all the jobs I had held prior had prepared me to take on that responsibility. In other words, I had been deliberately developed to take on this new role.

That was the first time I encountered and discussed the process of development. Often throughout the rest of my career, even as a senior officer, I started to understand why I was receiving certain assignments. For example, when I was assigned to be Chief of Staff of the Combined Air Operations Center (CAOC), I realized my leadership wanted me to learn the operational level of war. I had never even been to the CAOC, let alone know what the chief of staff or the staff actually did. Later, I was chosen to be the Air Force Vice Chief of Staff's senior executive officer in the Pentagon despite having yet to have an assignment to the

Pentagon in my career. The purpose was for me to learn how the Air Force Headquarters staff worked and the issues they were facing. Then, shockingly, I was assigned to US Space Command. I was a helicopter pilot for most of my career, and now I was going to be a senior leader in space operations. I didn't realize that this assignment prepared me for a year-long deployment to Operation Inherent Resolve, where the knowledge of space operations would prove critical. All along the way, I was deliberately developed for more responsibility.

During my Air Force career, I cannot begin to count my conversations and discussions regarding how we identify, select and train young talent to become future leaders. Many confuse mentoring and deliberate development. Mentoring is what I refer to as charity—everyone should have a leader mentor and be able to connect with those leaders who have experiences to share. Mentoring is free advice to help individuals develop goals and desires. I have had—and continue to have—several mentors with differing experiences. Deliberate development is a process that prepares individuals for more responsibility within an organization. Individuals who stand out above their peers are selected to be deliberately developed. They receive increased responsibility which, of course, leads to more opportunities to succeed or fail. Those who succeed continue to be identified for further development, and those that struggle may be revectored to other jobs that more appropriately match their skills. In the end, this process will produce leaders who have been prepared, trained, and have received the right experiences to take on increased responsibilities within the organization.

As leaders, it is important to understand the difference between mentoring and the deliberate development of individuals. When leaders understand the difference, they are more prepared and equipped to grow their organization's next generation of leaders.

TAKEAWAYS

- Mentoring is free advice for everyone.
- Deliberate development is a measured process.
- Deliberate development is how we grow the next generation of leaders.

Figure 3-1: The Author, 66th Rescue Squadron Commander, during Operation Iraqi Freedom, Balad Air Base, Iraq, 2007

Figure 3-2: The Author, Deputy Commanding General, during Operation Inherent Resolve, Baghdad, Iraq, 2018

Figure 3-3: The Author, Deputy Commanding General for Operations, during Operation Inherent Resolve, Syria/Iraq border, 2019

Figure 3-4: The Author, 15th Air Force Commander, takes the final flight for aircraft 009 that was flown to rescue downed stealth pilot during Operation Allied Force, Hurlburt Field, Florida, 2021

PART 4

ROB POLUMBO

RETIRED MAJOR GENERAL ROB "MUMBLES" POLUMBO is a senior consultant with Two Blue Aces, LLC. After 33 years of service, he retired as the special assistant to the commander, US Air Force Reserve Command, Robins Air Force Base. He assisted and advised the commander on the daily operations of the command, consisting of approximately 70,000 citizen airmen and more than 300 aircraft among three numbered air forces. He is also Jake Polumbo's brother.

"Rob has outlined for us all a foundation and path to apply years of proven techniques that have led to positive results. I lived 'line abreast' with Rob for many years, and I find his ability to take his life's testimony and clearly capture and formulate principles fascinating. These pillars work and thrive in a classroom, a ball field, our homes, a fighter squadron, and any Fortune 100 company. Our society thirsts for tools like this to make our world a better place. I've witnessed his commitment to the ideals he outlines in his marriage, fatherhood, brotherhood, and service to the nation and the community. Rob does not rest because he sees where we all need encouragement and guidance on how to address one of the core character traits that this entire nation needs—leadership. Flying a fighter jet is reserved for a select few; applying fighter pilot principles of success can be done by anyone. Rob details this for us all in this tremendous account of how it was done and, more importantly, how it can be done by you. It's time to plant and harvest some corn. Read on!"

Phil Dismukes

CEO and Founder, BGI

CHAPTER 16

FOLLOWERSHIP IS THE KEY

"He who cannot be a good follower, cannot be a good leader." —Aristotle

---

AS I REFLECT on my path through life, much of it seems like a blur in the rear-view mirror, with occasional moments of reflection to grasp the meaning of significant events. But one stage of the ride will always be etched in my mind as the most decisive event of my life. I grew up a military brat moving from place to place until I was six years old when my Dad retired from the Air Force, and my family settled in the small town of Winter Haven, Florida. My childhood was consumed with participating in every sport I could pack in outside the hours I spent going to school. My first goal was to be perfect at everything. However, I quickly figured out that trying to be perfect in an imperfect world was a futile pursuit. So, I throttled back *just a little* to strive to be above average in most endeavors.

My dream as a kid was to grow up to be an NFL quarterback. Two things hindered my progress—I never grew past five feet, nine inches, and I wasn't very good at the game. As reality quickly set in, my Dad helped me along by asking me what I would do when he "invited" me to move out of the house after high school. After overcoming the shock of *this* revelation, I decided I would show the world what I could do, and I followed my big brother to the United States Air Force Academy in Colorado Springs. Retiring from the Air Force 37 years later and living ten men's lives of adventures, I look back and acknowledge this one decision led to the most important experience in my life.

Why would I elevate this leadership experience above all others, including an F-16 fighter pilot, operational test pilot, squadron commander during Operation Iraqi Freedom, general officer, airline pilot, consultant, husband, and father of two sons? The reason is simple—this is where I built the foundation of followership which would transcend every aspect of my personal and professional life.

No talk on leadership can begin without a thorough understanding of followership. My introduction started out much like everyone else's. The early experiences began at home with my siblings, competing with my peers on countless sports teams and navigating through a decade and a half of grade school indoctrination. My parents, coaches, and teachers all seemed to want the same behavior standard, which didn't fit well with my self-centered agenda. At one point in my academic career, a teacher was so frustrated with my antics he put me and my desk inside a refrigerator box and located me in the back of the classroom for a semester. This was my first introduction to the *penalty box*, and definitely not my last. My parents gave coaches permission to *exercise* the demons out of me by making me run extra laps and complete hundreds of extra calisthenics before, during, and after practice.

I'm sure by now you've figured out I was a *troubled* lad who needed to shape up. So, my Dad and older brother concocted a scheme to get me to volunteer to go to a military academy and get my mind right. The plan was to fly me out to the foothills of the Rockies, have my brother Dennis "drive-by" the US Air Force Academy (USAFA), and then take me snow skiing the rest of the weekend. Well, I fell for it! It was the best trip of my teenage years, and I was positive the Academy was for me even though I never saw the campus. I know my Dad is still grinning in his grave, and my brother still snickers when I tell the story of their conspiracy. This was the most important turning point of my life.

The Academy was touted as a leadership laboratory, but I found it to be more of a team training center. USAFA has always been referred to as *The Zoo* because of the huge crowds that would gather on the elevated viewing area by the chapel to observe the cadets march around the enormous, open terrazzo. From the very first day after arriving, the mission of the upperclassmen was to snuff out any individualism and develop the new class of freshmen into a team of dedicated followers. Everything we were taught centered around serving the team and its mission. This was a hard pill to swallow for most after being the valedictorians and most-likely-to-succeeds coming out of high school. Being called a "doolie" (which comes from the Greek word *doulos* or slave) did not conjure up feelings of success OR a bright future. And, somehow, this spartan lifestyle and subservient daily regimen significantly changed my self-centered outlook on the world.

The most general definition of followership is *the capacity or willingness to follow a leader*. The Academy, in excruciating detail, taught me the specifics of being a good follower by developing characteristics, skills, and an attitude worthy of the team. Here are a few of those skills ingrained in me during those four years:

- Act with ethical and moral character; integrity first.
- Be on time and prepared; disciplined.
- Strive to be the subject matter expert; attention to detail.
- Be a teammate with passion and drive; daily excellence.
- Build relationships with peers and supervisors; humble and approachable.
- Be loyal to your teammates and the mission; selfless service.

The first two years at the Zoo were filled with activities to build up the foundation of followership. One of the most valuable experiences was observing individuals in leadership positions through the lens of a fledgling follower. My impression of *some* of my early leaders was not favorable because it appeared they had forgotten the tenants of followership I was expected to live by. When I observed their actions, they no longer exhibited the most basic characteristics of a professional. They no longer followed the spartan lifestyle of character, honor, and virtue, which they readily demanded of their team. I was confused why we were told to do one thing while individuals in supervisory positions no longer conformed to the team's standards. In these situations, I noticed the team was alienated, unmotivated, disrespectful to their leader, and ultimately unsuccessful. On the other end of the spectrum, leaders that continued to develop their followership skills—even during their roles as leaders—developed united, motivated, respectful, and highly successful groups.

During my final two years at the Academy, I was placed in leadership positions culminating as the commander of a cadet squadron during my senior year. I made two major conclusions during my six-month test of leading 100 of my peers. First, the most impactful thing a leader can do is set an example for others to follow. Never ask your team to do something you are unwilling to do yourself. Second and most important, a leader will most likely spend a good portion of time in a follower role to HIS or her supervisor. When I graduated from the Academy in 1984, I packed my bags and took this watershed moment as the most important lesson I learned in my young life.

My next progression in leadership was in the team dynamics of a fighter pilot. I started out as a wingman—the ultimate follower role. After years of flying with many different flight leaders and observing their leadership—and followership—styles, I compared and contrasted their techniques with each team's overall performance. The data overwhelmingly showed that humble, approachable, and credible leaders were far more likely to lead successful teams than those who had forgotten their followership skills. I changed assignments numerous times over my 33-year career, leading groups and being part of teams ranging from just three individuals to organizations with over 70,000 people. After integrating within a new unit, I could tell quickly whether I had become part of a high-performance team just by watching how the unit interacted with each other. Through their respect and pursuit of the skills of a follower, I could sense the team had a solid leadership foundation and with it a great leader at the helm. My respect and admiration for those leaders came mostly because they never forgot their humble beginnings and understood the key to leadership is an unending foundation in followership.

I end this chapter with a couple of questions: Where did you develop your follower skills? Do you still try to improve them at every level of your progression? Do you practice them every day in your role as a leader?

TAKEAWAYS

- Great followers make the best leaders.
- Always be humble, approachable, and credible.
- Never stop developing your followership skills.

CHAPTER 17

THE 6Ps AND 3Rs

"You always pass failure on your way to success."
—Mickey Rooney

OVER MY 40 YEARS of professional life, including jobs in the Air Force, American Airlines, small businesses, consulting, and volunteer work with veterans, the most frequently asked question by far has been: "*What is your recipe for success?*" Early on, I didn't have a well-thought-out answer and usually just used the same old stale adage, "*I worked hard.*" As a leader, you will often be asked this question, so having a polished, coherent message will instill confidence that you know what success looks like at every level. I suggest a simple and easily remembered pitch will reinforce the essentials for a path to success for any endeavor. Here is what I came up with through observing hundreds of very successful individuals in all lines of work and all ages—the "**6Ps**" for success!

THE SIX Ps.

The first **P** is **PLAN**. In this highly competitive and complex world, you must have a detailed roadmap for your journey through life. Many of you had to plan to get through school and land a job. However, it doesn't end there—that's just the start of the sequence of events to a life of success. Periodically, you need to update your short- and long-term goals and devise a new, follow-on **PLAN** to achieve them. **PLANNING** never ends; it's a continuous process requiring thought-provoking time and effort. Don't be afraid to ask others for help and advice on your **PLAN**.

My next **P** is for **PASSION**. Once you have a **PLAN**, you must put your whole being into it—mind, body, and soul. It must be your focus each and every day. Everything you do, from the most mundane of tasks to the most complicated of projects, should be done with diligence and discipline. **PASSION** never takes a day off.

My third **P** is **PERSISTENCE** which is essential to sustain your **PASSION** and complete your **PLAN**. You will need plenty of this **P** to get through life and career challenges. Sure, there will be setbacks, deviations, detours, and delays, but your **PERSISTENCE** will keep you on track. Never give up!

The next **P** has given me the most difficulty during my journey, and it must be handled very delicately—

PERFECTION. Many of your efforts in life demand the highest standards of daily excellence and attention to detail. With 60 years of life experience, I have come to the conclusion that you should always strive for **PERFECTION**, tempered with the understanding that everything will not always go just as you **PLANNED.** So, if you give it everything you have and fall a little short, relish in your accomplishment and write off your frustration to an imperfect world. Never give up on the tenets of **PERFECTION.**

The next **P** makes all the other **Ps** sustainable and is crucial to your ability to perform at your highest level—being **PHYSICALLY** fit. Being fit includes the health and nourishment of the three pillars of your well-being—mind, body, and soul. Nothing has been more important for me to stay **PERFECTLY** on **PLAN** with **PASSION** and **PERSISTENCE** than by remaining **PHYSICALLY** fit. It should be a daily priority, not only for your health and well-being but also to set an example for your team. At the very least, you should carve out at least an hour each day to get the mind racing, the heart pumping, and the soul searching. Never forget to keep your mind, body, and soul **PHYSICALLY** fit!

And, last but not least—have **PHUN**. (I needed another **P** and was never a good speller anyway.) Always make time along the journey to enjoy life with your family and friends. Taking time off to recharge your batteries is not only healthy but is essential to your continued success. A life adventure without **PHUN** will end up being a long, arduous grind leaving you empty and unfulfilled. Never forget to put a little **PHUN** on your weekly schedule.

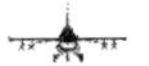

THE THREE Rs.

Now, for the tougher question, you will entertain more infrequently, but it will have a huge impact on you and your team's future success— *"what are the steps to recover from failure?"* All of us will inevitably face a time where we just didn't measure up and consequently let someone down, be it a customer or someone on our team. Not to worry, there is a clear and concise way to get back on track—all you have to do is remember the "**3Rs**".

First and foremost, you must **RECOGNIZE** your behavior, actions, or performance was not up to standards, and it was **your** fault. Sometimes we don't stop to evaluate our role in a blunder, and someone has to call us out, which can be an embarrassing moment. During these instances, we usually make excuses or quibble our way out of taking responsibility for the error. Next time—stop, think, and reflect. If it's your fault, own it immediately. The faster you fess up and acknowledge it was your fault, the quicker you will start the process of fixing the situation.

Next, you must have **REMORSE** for your actions. The definition is simple—be genuinely sorry for your actions! If you dropped the ball on an assignment or hurt someone's feelings, a personal apology will certainly turn the failure into a team-building moment and will reinforce the mutual respect of your co-workers. Nothing festers in a group worse than not making a timely, genuine apology to a teammate.

Lastly, you must **REHABILITATE** yourself in some form. Sometimes, this comes from a debrief, an admonishment, or a demotion from your boss, but many times it takes the form of a conscious self-adjustment on how you conduct yourself in the future. Accept the conditions of the rehabilitation without resentment or bitterness and capture the experience into a life lesson to prevent making the same error in the future. Always use the rehabilitation phase as a time to improve yourself and your performance.

I'd like to provide two examples of failures I encountered while I was the commander of a fighter squadron. The two individuals were US Air Force officers with the responsibility of piloting multimillion-dollar aircraft and setting examples for the rest of the Airmen in our unit. One individual was arrested for a DUI, and the other was accused of illegal drug use.

I became aware of these serious situations in very different circumstances. The pilot arrested for DUI came forward immediately after it occurred and informed me of the event. He **RECOGNIZED** his failure to uphold the standards of his position, **REMORSEFULLY** apologized for letting the squadron down, and immediately accepted the **REHABILITATION** measures the Air Force levied on all DUI offenders. During his six months in the penalty box, his daily excellence never waned, and he never complained about the disciplinary actions set against him. He successfully remained with the squadron for the rest of his career and was one of the most respected officers in the unit. He failed forward!

I was notified of the other pilot's alleged drug use only after a number of anonymous phone calls to the squadron were concealed by the individual, and a subsequent call was made to my supervisor. I conducted an investigation for these serious allegations as required by Air Force policy. Although the lab work proved negative for illegal drugs, the investigation uncovered eyewitness accounts alleging his drug use and presence at known locations where drug use was prevalent, according to law enforcement reports. In addition, the individual had conspired with his supervisor to cover up the incident by not informing me of his girlfriend's calls to the squadron about drug use. With no hard evidence of drug use besides the testimony of a few of his estranged friends, I confronted the individual on the situation. The officer did not **RECOGNIZE** the gravity of this poor judgment and how his indiscretion reflected unfavorably on the high standards our nation requires of our military. He was not in the least bit **REMORSEFUL** for exercising behavior unbecoming of an officer by continually being in the presence of individuals using illegal drugs and conspiring to cover up the situation with his supervisor. When I took administrative actions to document his poor judgment, he refused to **REHABILITATE** and did not return to being a productive member of the unit. He could have salvaged this failure by acknowledging his poor judgment, accepting the administrative action, and changing his attitude. Although I tried to coach him through this situation, he elected to disregard the **3Rs** and never recovered from this failure.

The **3Rs** are clear and concise, but I didn't say they were easy.

Human nature can make us reluctant to admit failure, express remorse, and pay dues for messing up. So, this must be a learned process, hopefully, started early in life. For many of us, the **3Rs** were used quite a bit when we were growing up because we were always in trouble. Our parents and teachers taught us the **3Rs** as an important part of the maturing process. As we grew older, admitting failure was a sign of weakness which resulted in the erosion of the benefits of the failure process. This left grievances unresolved, improvement in performance stagnant, and definitely impacted our relationship with others. You must know how to succeed and fail; both are essential to developing life lessons that will improve your and your teammate's performance both personally and professionally. As a leader, you will not only be faced with failures of your own to remedy but also intervention in the failures of your teammates. Some individuals will need a refresher on the **3Rs** to get back on track to the **6Ps** of success!

TAKEAWAYS

- Develop your own personal guide to success and failure.
- A good leader knows the road to success.
- Always fail forward.

CHAPTER 18

KNOW YOUR CUSTOMER

"Customer service shouldn't just be a department; it should be the entire company." —Tony Hsieh

THERE I WAS... my four-ship of fighters was flying at 600 mph at 300 feet above the ground in mountainous terrain on our way to a target that could only be seen through our navigation pods using infrared technology. It was the middle of the night with no moon illumination, and as we used to say in the fighter business: "it was darker than the inside of a cow belly!" Our canopies were filled with a sea of darkness as we flew through valleys and ravines with unseen mountain peaks thousands of feet above. We relied totally on our F-16's terrain-following radar to keep us from hitting the rocks. I placed my wingmen in a trail formation with three miles of spacing between each aircraft to prevent us from running into each other as we maneuvered through the terrain. We avoided known threats by planning a low-level route that hid us from detection by enemy radars using direct and indirect terrain masking. When enemy aircraft and ground threats presented themselves, my team would maneuver to successfully defeat their deadly missile attacks. When the target approached, the intensity of the mission reached its peak. In a matter of a minute and a half, each pilot executed a fly-up attack profile to find, fix, track, and engage the target, which inherently exposed the aircraft to detection by enemy threats. During the delivery of the weapon, each pilot had to pull up away from the ground and "throw" the bombs about five miles at the intended target. Once the bombs were released, the most dangerous 30 seconds of the mission commenced with guiding the bomb by maintaining the targeting pod laser spot on the target while simultaneously flying the aircraft back down to 300 feet to minimize exposure to the threat. After viewing the detonation of the bomb in the targeting pod, each pilot assessed whether their bombs destroyed their target. The four-ship reformed into the planned formation and flew back through the mountains to friendly territory. I never flew more demanding, high-intensity missions in my Air Force career.

The time was just after Operation Desert Storm when we successfully made Saddam Hussein's army retreat from Kuwait in a 43-day campaign. Our strategy for waging war was still focused on Cold War tactics of flying fighters at low altitude below the enemy's radar detection and tracking capabilities. With the addition of terrain-following radar and precision-guided bombs, new tactics needed to be developed for the improved technology on our fighter force. The team I was on at the 422 Test and Evaluation Squadron at Nellis Air Force Base, Nevada, was charged with developing the updated tactics manual. Our job was to determine how to successfully execute this very demanding mission with the F-16 Low Altitude Navigation and Targeting Infrared for Night (LANTIRN) system. We flew this scenario hundreds of times to determine the best tactics, techniques, and procedures (TTP) to ensure a brand new, qualified F-16 pilot could successfully complete this mission—and do it again the next night. Our overall responsibility was to the Air Force, but the ultimate customer was the newest wingman in the F-16 community. We all knew the customer well because we were the newest wingman just a decade before. We were completely devoted to making this mission *survivable* for Blue 4 *(the most inexperienced member of the four-ship was referred to as Blue 4)*. As a young captain, this notion of "knowing your customer" would become a critical part of my leadership foundation throughout the rest of my career.

My first introduction to customer service came in the 1980s when the Department of Defense latched on to the Total Quality Management (TQM) business strategy. Like any new program, it was met with immediate resistance, and many units didn't embrace the two key concepts of customer service and continuous improvement process. Looking back at it as a young fighter pilot,

I didn't understand how a business strategy could be useful to a military organization. After all, most would argue the word customer only had meaning in describing a business relationship between someone who sells goods and services to another individual. As far as I could tell, I wasn't selling anything to anyone at this time in my career. But what I didn't realize at the time was the relationship between a flight lead and a wingman is the epitome of the customer service model.

Only after flying countless missions as both a leader and a wingman did I finally make the connection that a customer relationship is simply a service contract from one individual to another. The key to the relationship is one person's performance serves or supports another's needs and requirements. Furthermore, I believe *everyone* has multiple customers, both internal and external to their organization, that count on them to fulfill critical tasks and activities. And within this customer web, each successive level of the process is charged with improving the product, thereby increasing overall customer satisfaction.

After realizing this broader spectrum of service to others, I started to look at each situation as a unique opportunity to best serve someone down, up, or sideways in the organization who depended on my performance to complete their tasks and do their job better. Many times, there were second and third-level customers who became apparent only by talking to the first-level customer I directly served.

Additionally, in many cases, both individuals in a relationship have customer responsibilities to the other. For example, supervisors and subordinates have specific service responsibilities to each other. The subordinate has the responsibility to fulfill the performance obligations required by his or her supervisor, while the same supervisor has a responsibility to provide the subordinate with the resources and training necessary to accomplish their tasks. If the leader of the team has instituted a culture of customer service and continuous improvement, there will be a synergistic increase in overall performance due to the constant refinement of the product at every level before it reaches the customer.

Paying attention to this network of customers is the heart of good leadership, and the key ingredient is daily excellence. The "customer first" concept thrives when each person on the team makes a concerted effort to improve the product, service, or performance at their level before sending it to the next. Customer service starts with the leader through the development of a culture of excellence and attention to detail. This culture has its foundation in the "Golden Rule" principle of treating others as you want to be treated. This is followed by a dedication to performing and delivering the best possible product or service to your customer. As the leader of your team, it is up to you to identify all of your customer relationships, both internal and external to the organization, determine what is required to deliver the best support, evaluate the customer's satisfaction and continuously make improvements to the process. Your team is essential to these duties and must be included in every aspect of customer service decisions because they know their immediate customers the best. If your process doesn't look like this, it's time to make it happen. If your business successfully models this, it's probably time to have a staff meeting to review and update your process. Continuous improvement is essential to good customer relations.

Now for the rest of the story about my *Blue 4* customer ... As we continued to perform operational testing of the new LANTIRN mission, lessons learned from Operation Desert Storm poured in, causing a debate over the strategy of flying at low altitude against an enemy with large numbers of man-portable air-defense systems (MANPADS), anti-aircraft artillery (AAA) and small arms (SA). This debate resulted over the fact that a number of our Airmen were shot down at low altitude by these threats during the short conflict. In the same time frame, test and training sorties back home flying against *simulated* threats were marred in blood, usually from ground impact due to task saturation during low-altitude maneuvering. After already losing one of the most experienced members of our test team to a ground impact, I can vividly remember a night we all came into the debrief from another demanding test sortie in which we almost lost another highly experienced brother to a collision with the ground. We all looked around the room and determined with resolve that these tactics were beyond the capability of *our customer*. If the most experienced pilots in the AF were running into the ground, then we would not be serving our community if we didn't make necessary changes to the TTPs to decrease the risk. The next morning, we informed our leaders that we needed to stand down and make changes to the test plan. The test was immediately put on hold.

After making changes to the TTPs, which significantly reduced the risk of a mishap, we finished the test and delivered the new tactics manual to the F-16 community. I'm convinced now that our advocacy for Blue 4 had not only saved lives but had an important impact on our leadership to change the future of fighter aviation. Obviously, getting a 700,000-person enterprise to change course took time, money, and effort, but over the course of the next decade, I saw our Air Force make advances in new all-weather precision weapons, improve suppression of enemy air-defense systems, and develop electronic warfare measures all aimed at being able to fly above the low-altitude threats and have higher success rates hitting our target. All of these technological advances allowed us to stop flying low which greatly reduce the risk of losing *Blue 4* in both combat and training missions. We knew our customer was counting on us, and we didn't let him down.

TAKEAWAYS

- It all starts with knowing your customer.
- Continuous improvement makes successful teams.
- Good leaders know the customer always comes *first.*

CHAPTER 19

TRUE GRIT—NO QUIT

"Grit, the raw endurance, perseverance and passion that keeps you going despite obstacles."
—Anonymous

"A balanced intellect presupposes a harmonious growth of body, mind and soul." —Mahatma Gandhi

AFTER READING the book *Endurance* about the truly incredible story of Sir Ernest Shackleton's 1914 failed attempt to cross the continent of Antarctica, I was reminded of the leadership attributes of fortitude, perseverance, courage, and commitment—the epitome of true grit. The book chronicles the voyage of a captain and a crew of 28 men who set sail from England to be the first to land on Antarctica and cross the continent on foot to the other coast. The expedition meets with adversity when the ship becomes engulfed in floating sea ice that thwarts their arrival on land. For the next two years, the captain and his crew endure every conceivable threat to their survival from exposure, starvation, and depression to finally break free from the ice and plot a course to safety. Through a culture of disciplined routine, impeccable planning/decision making, mutual trust, and work ethic, EVERYONE survived the two-year odyssey. My takeaway from this story is that mental, physical, and spiritual toughness held this team together, and the true grit of the leader inspired it!

My earlier chapter listed **PASSION**, **PERSISTENCE**, and **PHYSICAL** fitness as keys to your road to success. These attributes require health and harmony in mind, body, and soul. As a leader, you are not only responsible for your well-being but also for inspiring your teammates on the importance of these three pillars of life.

I believe most leaders today don't see "true grit" as an integral part of a successful team because it is no longer emphasized in our homes, schools, communities, or workplaces. We have become a soft, self-centered, impatient society ready to cut and run at the first signs of adversity or discomfort. Instead of confronting challenges, determining a new course of action, and rolling up our sleeves to get after it, we submit to blaming others for our misfortune and believing we are victims unable to change the direction of our organization. When this lack of resilience emanates from the leadership, it acts as a contagion that rapidly moves through every level of the team. Instead of being tough, committed, and courageous, we fall into the trap of complacency, pessimism, and minimum effort. Standards are lowered, and the team falls onto a slippery slope of self-pity and waning performance. If you've been in an organization like this, you know this is a recipe for failure.

Developing true grit should start early in life and should be reinforced over a lifetime pursuit of daily excellence. The ingredients of grit and toughness are acquired first at home through the learned attributes of discipline, regiment, responsibility, accountability, resilience, work ethic, perseverance, determination, and fortitude. Parenting is the most important leadership position we will ever have in our lives. We are responsible for developing the next generation of productive citizens and leaders. Many times, we confuse care and love with coddling. Coddling is the act of doing something for individuals who should do the task for themselves. By making a child or young adult do for themselves, the seeds of self-reliance and resilience are planted. Coddling only acts to relieve the person of their sense of ownership for the outcome of their actions and makes them less likely to put in the effort necessary to adapt and overcome obstacles. This leads to an "entitled" society where the terms **earned** and **deserved** are erroneously used interchangeably. Today, average performance or just showing up "deserves" a ribbon. No one deserves anything unless it were truly earned through daily diligence and excellence.

This strong foundation is only the beginning of the journey to true grit. Through a whole host of pursuits, including education, training, athletics, careers, and community activity, we are continually challenged to adapt and overcome adversity by developing mental, physical, and spiritual toughness. This development doesn't end at a certain age and should be the fire that burns inside our bellies throughout our lives.

How does a leader inspire their teammates to maintain wellness in mind, body, and soul? The first key comes from my chapter on "knowing your customer!" I made it a point to get to know my teammates, both personally and professionally. When a new individual was assigned to the team, I took the time to talk with them about their background, goals, strengths, weaknesses, and how I could help them succeed. I followed up with the individual's immediate supervisor and recurring evaluation reviews. Once I knew what made the individual tick, I could better tailor my approach to inspiring them to build true grit. Here are a few ideas I used to inspire individuals in each pillar of life.

- Mind. Challenge with further education and training linked to their goals; suggest books aligned with their interests; inspire objective debate on topics; ask for viable solutions to problems; assign to be project lead.
- Body. Suggest physical activity aligned with their interest; instigate pursuit of long-term physical goals; challenge with friendly competition.

- Soul. Challenge to develop faith in *something*—friends, family, team, community, higher-being; participate in charity and volunteer activities.

Leaders should also seek inspiration for their team by inviting individuals who have endured great adversity and challenges in their personal and professional lives to share their story. They can be found in your organization, in companies you do business with, or read about in books like Shackleton's book *Endurance*. Additionally, I would reach out to our nation's greatest wealth of true grit—our military veterans and first responders. These individuals are perfect mentors and role models who have been placed in austere and dire situations where true grit and credible leadership were the only way their team (or customer) thrived and survived. Most, if not all, will tell you that the courage and commitment of their leader was the most important ingredient to their success.

The most powerful inspiration a leader can provide his co-workers is to practice what you preach. Setting the example and maintaining a healthy balance of the three pillars is always the most compelling way to inspire your group to do the same. Don't be the leader who fails to match the talk with the walk in both your personal and professional life. This is why YOU must always emanate true grit before YOU can inspire others. Mental, physical, and spiritual toughness doesn't happen overnight but rather is a lifetime pursuit forged over many trials, tribulations, and failures. Only those who continually get back on their feet and recommit to daily excellence find more success than failure. True grit is the epitome of the human spirit and should always be inspired in your team.

One of the most rewarding endeavors I've ever been a part of has been helping our veterans recover from the visible and invisible wounds incurred over the past 30 years of war in Southwest Asia. Through *The 22 Project*, veterans with traumatic brain injury (TBI) and post-traumatic stress disorder (PTSD) are brought to Delray Beach, Florida, for hyperbaric oxygen therapy (HBOT). A Single Photon Emission Computed Tomography (SPECT) of the brain is administered to the veterans before and after the HBOT treatments to analyze the improvement in blood flow and activity of different areas of the brain. Over a 30-day period, the veteran receives 40 one-hour chamber sessions breathing 100% oxygen in a higher-than-normal pressure environment. The positive effects on the brain, including increased blood flow and neural activity in injured areas, have been astounding. But the secret sauce to this program is not just the improvement of the body; it's the targeting of the two other pillars of wellness. Through weekly Christian fellowship meetings and outdoor activities, a group of grey-beard volunteers bring the vets back into the fold by inspiring their road to recovery by also including their mind and soul. The veterans leave south Florida with an optimistic outlook and focused commitment to maintaining their renewed personal wellness. There is no better inspiration than seeing your team rise up from adversity to new levels of success. A well-balanced and motivated organization will have the grit to endure any challenge. Never quit!

TAKEAWAYS

- True grit starts with the leader.
- Personal wellness includes the mind, body, and soul.
- Teams with true grit overcome all challenges and never quit.

CHAPTER 20

GROWING YOUR SEED CORN

> "Plant a seed of greatness in your children. Speak a word of encouragement to someone who needs to hear it. Inspire someone to be a better person. One day you'll reap a harvest, and your world will become a better place to live." —George Foreman

---

CORN IS ONE OF THE MOST DIFFICULT CROPS to plant, maintain and sustain. Every variable, from soil content, temperature, moisture, nourishment, and protection from disease, has stringent parameters in the four-stage process (plant, germinate, vegetate, and reproduce) to successfully grow corn year after year. In addition, corn is wind-pollinated, so it must be planted near other corn plants to allow cross-pollination to ensure the best genetics for success. So, too, does cultivating new seed corn in your organization. It requires a well-thought-out plan, precise ingredients, diverse pollination, teamwork, and timely execution to continuously grow the next leaders of the team. I told you in my first chapter what was the most important experience that planted my seed on rich leadership soil. Now, I want to tell you what inspired me to sprout and establish a deep and solid foundation for becoming a leader.

My introduction to the fighter aviation business was the most instrumental part of my development into new seed corn for the Air Force and the rest of my professional career. As a wingman, I was challenged daily by my flight leads to become an outstanding follower. Each mission we flew was meticulously planned, briefed, executed, and then thoroughly debriefed. Many times, the debrief lasted longer than the planning, briefing, and flying mission combined. Lessons learned were always summarized at the end of the entire process, so they were fresh in our minds for the next day's mission. This "lather, rinse, repeat" methodology developed a foundation of habit-forming processes that became the core foundation of approaching any situation or decision matrix. My immediate supervisors were charged with my daily growth and provided the cross-pollination of different leadership styles to meld into the best formula for my development.

The culmination of my immersion into becoming the next generation leader for the Air Force came when I attended the

Fighter Weapons Instructor Course at Nellis AFB, Nevada. Only one percent of the entire aviation community has the opportunity to attend the course. A key objective is to make every member of the team part of the cultivation process of developing new leaders for the Air Force. The pollination of diverse ideas, methods, and examples produced a hardened, survivable seed ready to take on any challenge. Every day our leaders demanded, developed, demonstrated, delegated, and debriefed excellence!

I previously outlined the baseline for instituting a good leadership foundation through embracing followership skills, learning how to succeed as well as recover from failure, knowing who you serve, and developing a team with true grit. Now I will tie it all together and discuss the key ingredients in setting your team apart from the rest of the competition. It is a simple concept but one that requires constant attention and vigilance from every member of the group. Everyone must feel intense, passionate accountability for the success of the team. In the military, we refer to this "feeling" as *esprit de corps*— "a sense of unity and of common interests and responsibilities as developed among a group of persons closely associated in a task, cause or enterprise." This commonality of cause comes from trust, mutual respect, and knowing one another very well. It is paramount these attributes originate and emanate from the leader. This type of work environment doesn't happen overnight but is cultivated over time through experiences and disciplined effort.

The success of this program rests solely on the leadership to set in motion a repeatable, continuous process to identify, train and develop the NexGen leaders for an organization. Some leaders see this as a threat to their own future, but if you think like George Foreman, the end result is the overall improvement of the world around us. Producing more competent, courageous, committed, compassionate, and character-filled individuals can only make your business more prosperous and our world a better place to live. How is this seed-producing ecosystem developed and sustained? Here are my "**5Ds**" for your team's leadership development.

THE FIVE Ds.

DEMAND TEAM STANDARDS. It is essential to establish core values that will illuminate a common path to success for your team. In the Air Force, integrity first, service before self, and excellence in all we do, guide the daily work ethic. Core values will lead to defined team standards developed by the leader. These standards are the essential ingredients used to make critical decisions, not only in our professional endeavors, but also in our personal lives. These core values and standards should become the heart and soul of the team and a non-negotiable requirement for every individual. I guarantee more success than failure will result from your team's incorporation of core values in their daily decision-making.

DEVELOP VISION. The leader's next step is to provide clarity of effort by providing a vision for success and the specific goals to get there. In the military, this was referred to as "commander's intent" and was the framework for centralized command, decentralized execution. Through clear goals, guidelines, and policies, the leader puts in place the architecture to allow the team to act on his or her intent rather than continually "check in" with the boss for guidance. Decentralized execution creates initiative and efficiency for a timelier execution of the game plan. Empowering your team to make decisions from your intent also builds core leadership skills for them to utilize when they become the boss.

DEMONSTRATE BY EXAMPLE. Once standards are set, it is up to YOU to set the example! Your team will watch to see if you live by the standards, you have set and WALK THE TALK in your professional and personal actions. Always lead from the front.

In my first chapter, I emphasized the paramount importance of the development of followership skills. It's worth repeating because your seed corn will always look to see if you continue developing these skills and never forget where you came from.

- Act with ethical and moral character.
- Be on time and prepared.
- Strive to be the subject matter expert.
- Be a teammate with passion and drive.
- Build relationships with peers and supervisors.
- Be loyal to your teammates and the mission.

DELEGATE TO THE MOST JUNIOR TEAM MEMBER. Delegation is one of the toughest areas for a leader to embrace because it entails relinquishing authority and incurring risk. But if done effectively, the team will reap the benefit of efficiency of effort, accountability at the most junior level, and development of new seed corn.

Delegation starts with getting to know each and every member of the team, both personally and professionally. My first action after becoming a leader of a new group was to gain insight into everyone's strengths, weaknesses, experience, and background. I used this information to make assessments of their followership skills, motivation for advancement, and capability to lead.

I then formulated a plan to delegate projects most aligned with their strengths and seek education and training venues to work on their weaknesses. Through performance reviews, I continually determine the best way to inspire, motivate, mentor, and build rapport with each individual to maximize their daily performance and develop a plan for their leadership progression.

DEBRIEF EVERYTHING. Nothing has had more impact on my development in leadership than capturing lessons learned from countless situations and experiences. Diligent and disciplined debriefing is essential to the growth of every member of the team. It should be as important as the planning, briefing, and execution of any project or game plan. Without it, a team will be less likely to understand the reasons a plan succeeded and more likely to repeat errors from a previous failure.

Debriefing provides an opportunity for the team to objectively evaluate performance on any project or activity. It is the single most important step in building continuous improvement and increasing the performance of your team.

TAKEAWAYS

- Provide clear vision, goals, and intent.
- Know your teammates and develop new seed corn.
- Demand, develop, demonstrate, delegate, and always debrief.

Figure 4-1: The Author's graduation day from the US Air Force Academy, receiving his commission from the Commander-in-Chief, President Reagan, 1984

Figure 4-2: Twenty-four years later and over 4000 hours...the Author flies his final flight in the F-16 *Fighting Falcon*, 2008

Figure 4-3: The Author flying over 74,000 feet above the earth in the U-2 *Dragon Lady*, 2008

Figure 4-4: The bus and the sports car-two careers at once...American Airlines first officer and US Air Force Reserve fighter pilot (1997-2017)

THE AUTHORS

CHAD FRANKS

RETIRED MAJOR GENERAL CHAD "SPARKY" FRANKS transitioned from the US Air Force after 31 years of dedicated active service. He culminated his career as the Commander, 15th Air Force, Shaw Air Force Base, South Carolina. General Franks was responsible for organizing, training, and equipping 13 wings and three direct reporting units in Air Combat Command ensuring operational readiness of over 800 aircraft and 47,000 Airmen.

General Franks was commissioned in 1990 as a graduate of the University of New Orleans Air Force ROTC program. He has served in a variety of flying positions during assignments in Air Force Special Operations Command, Air Education and Training

Command, and Air Combat Command. Franks is a decorated command pilot with more than 3200 flying hours in the MH-60G, HH-60G, HC-130, and T-37 including combat hours flown in Europe and Southwest Asia.

Franks has served in several high-profile positions including Chief of Staff for the Combined Forces Air Component Commander in Southwest Asia, Senior Executive Officer to the Air Force Vice Chief of Staff, Vice Commander Fourteenth Air Force in Air Force Space Command, and Deputy Commanding General for Operations and Intelligence, Operation Inherent Resolve in Baghdad, Iraq. He has commanded at the numbered Air Force, wing, group, and squadron level. He has deployed in support of Operations Provide Comfort, Northern Watch, Allied Force, Iraqi Freedom, and Inherent Resolve.

General Franks' area of expertise includes operations, strategic development, risk management, team building, leading large organizations, and change management. He was awarded a master's degree in Strategy Studies from the US Army War College as well as a master's degree in Military Operational Art and Science from the US Air Force Air Command and Staff College.

Chad and his wife, Kim, of over 32 years, reside in Monument, Colorado. Their oldest son, Logan, and his wife Carla, live in Valdosta, Georgia, where he is an ICU nurse. Chad and Kim's youngest son, Tyler, lives in Denver, Colorado, and works for a nationally known advertising company.

LARRY MARTIN

RETIRED MAJOR GENERAL LARRY MARTIN transitioned from the Air Force after 32 years of active service. He is a Senior Consultant with Two Blue Aces and specializes in guiding large organizations with enterprise-level strategic planning; building international, government, industry, and community alliances; driving process improvement; and steering talent management and leadership training.

Prior to his military retirement, Larry served as the Assistant Deputy Under Secretary of the Air Force, where he oversaw 226 Washington DC-based employees managing Air Force international matters with US government, industry partners and over 100 worldwide air forces. He returned to Tampa, site of his MacDill Air Force Base command, with his wife, Julia, in 2017. He and Julia have two sons, J.J., an Army military police officer and Jeff, a Space Force intelligence officer.

He is a command pilot with over 3,700 hours in the C-130E/H/J, KC-135R/T, E-8, UV-18B and C-37A aircraft, commanded at the squadron and wing-level, served in Southwest Asia, taught history at the US Air Force Academy, and held leadership assignments at Air Mobility Command, US Pacific Command, US Transportation Command and Headquarters, United States Air Force, Washington, D.C. A distinguished graduate of the US Air Force Academy, Squadron Officer School, and the Marine Corps Command and Staff College, he graduated with highest academic distinction from the Air War College.

As a part of the Two Blue Aces team, his work has ranged from executive coaching and team building for a major port, a strategy review for a nationally recognized third-party logistics company, contract consulting for defense services providers, guiding US government and overseas services business expansion for defense and defense service companies and leadership programs for military units and area universities.

Deeply committed to the Tampa Bay region, he serves on the Board of Directors for the Tampa Bay Defense Alliance, the Royal Air Force Museum American Foundation board, the University of South Florida's World Advisory Council and served as the volunteer President for the Medal of Honor Convention Tampa Bay 2019.

H.D. "JAKE" POLUMBO

RETIRED MAJOR GENERAL H.D. "JAKE" POLUMBO is a founding partner and senior consultant for Two Blue Aces, LLC, a leadership firm that specializes in strategic reviews, business plan development, leadership training, and mentoring. His primary focus is in the defense and aerospace sectors, with an emphasis on leadership and business networking.

In 2015, after 34 years of service, Jake retired from the US Air Force as the commander of the Ninth Air Force in South Carolina, comprising eight active-duty wings in the southeastern United States with more than 450 aircraft and over 29,000 active-duty and civilian personnel.

He entered active duty as a graduate of the US Air Force Academy in 1981 and commanded at the squadron, group, and three times at the wing level. He served in strategic planning positions in Europe as the Director of Strategy and plans at US Africa Command and in the Pentagon as the Assistant Deputy Director for Global Operations on the Joint Staff. General Polumbo also served as a task force commander in Afghanistan in 2012. He attended the Federal Executive Institute and was a Senior Fellow at Georgetown University's Institute for the Study of Diplomacy.

A decorated command pilot, Jake logged over 3,000 flying hours in all models of the F-16 and holds the distinction as the first and only US Air Force general officer to fly the U-2S in combat, completing 21 missions in Operations Enduring Freedom and Iraqi Freedom.

Jake is a former Chair of the Central Florida Development Council Board of Directors and serves as an advisor to the president of Florida Polytechnic University in Lakeland, Florida. He is active in the local general aviation community, is a Certified Flight Instructor Instrument in single and multi-engine land aircraft as well as an instructor pilot in single-engine seaplanes. Jake is co-author of *Leadership from 30,000 feet* published in 2019.

Jake and his wife Sandra, a Florida native, have been married for 42 years. Their oldest son, Chad, is a lieutenant colonel in the US Air Force with his wife, Julie, and they have two sons, Nolan, and Garrett. Jake and Sandra's youngest son, Erik, lives in Virginia with his wife, Alexine, where they run four businesses together.

ROB POLUMBO

RETIRED MAJOR GENERAL ROB "MUMBLES" POLUMBO transitioned from the US Air Force after 33 years of service in 2017. His career culminated as the special assistant to the commander, US Air Force Reserve Command, Robins Air Force Base. General Polumbo assisted and advised the commander on the daily operations of the command, consisting of approximately 70,000 citizen airmen and more than 300 aircraft among three numbered Air Forces, providing air, space, and cyber support to combatant commands worldwide.

Maj Gen Rob Polumbo was a distinguished graduate of the US Air Force Academy in 1984. During his 14 years of active duty, he served as an F-16 instructor pilot, flight examiner, weapons officer, operational test and evaluation pilot, operations officer, and commander. He was a member of the 422 Test and Evaluation Squadron and flew as a project test pilot in numerous tactics development evaluations for the F-16. He also was the commander of 57 WG/Det 2 conducting foreign materiel exploitation. Additionally, he served as the aide-de-camp to the Air Force Chief of Staff. He transitioned to the Air Force Reserve Command in 1997 and joined the 482nd Fighter Wing at Homestead ARB. He flew F-16s in the 93rd Fighter Squadron, served as commander of the unit and later as the 482nd Fighter Wing Vice Commander. His senior executive positions included mobilization assistant to numerous commands including the Air Force Warfare Center, Air Combat Command, 7th and 12th Air Forces and Headquarters Air Force. His areas of expertise include joint all-domain command and control operations, tactics development and evaluation, foreign materiel exploitation, commercial aviation and leadership and character development.

Rob is a command pilot with more than 4,300 hours of military aviation time in all blocks of the F-16 and YF-112D, including combat operations in Southwest Asia. He also graduated from the US Air Force Fighter Weapons Instructor Course in 1991. During his 23-year American Airline's career, he logged more than 9,800 flying hours in B727, B757, B767 and B777 aircraft. He earned a master's degree in Aviation Science from Embry-Riddle University in 1994. Currently, Rob is a senior consultant for Two Blue Aces consulting group; executive associate for the South Florida Defense Alliance; and volunteers for *The 22 Project*, a non-profit organization providing support for veterans with traumatic brain injuries. Rob is co-author of *Leadership from 30,000 feet* published in 2019. He is married to the former Claudia Barriga of Miami, FL and they have two sons. Their oldest son, Jake, is a F-16 fighter pilot in the US Air Force. Zach is a senior at the US Naval Academy and will be commissioned a 2nd lieutenant in the US Marine Corps.

NOTES

CHAPTER 1: LEADERSHIP, INTEGRITY, AND THE RIGHT THING

1. Carl A Posey, "50 Years of Hercules, As utilitarian as a bucket and just as plain, Lockheed's C-130 has flown almost everything to almost everywhere," Smithsonian Magazine, September 2004, https://www.smithsonianmag.com/air-space-magazine/50-years-of-hercules-5504946/

CHAPTER 2: THE CASE FOR NUMBER 2

1. Lin-Manuel Miranda, "Right Hand Man" from *Hamilton: An American Musical,* https://genius.com/Christopher-jackson-lin-manuel-miranda-leslie-odom-jr-and-original-broadway-cast-of-hamilton-right-hand-man-lyrics
2. Kristin Roberts and David Morgan, Editing by Chris Wilson, "U.S. B-1 bomber catches fire in Qatar, crew unhurt," Reuters, April 4, 2008, https://www.reuters.com/article/us-usa-qatar-crash/u-s-b-1-bomber-catches-fire-in-qatar-crew-unhurt-idUSWBT00870920080404
3. The Associated Press, "Officials: Man who tried entering base was AWOL," The Gazette, June 15, 2010, https://gazette.com/news/officials-man-who-tried-entering-base-was-awol/article_1dddae09-0623-50bb-b4ce-5821c7dc34a2.html

CHAPTER 3: LEADING AN INTERNATIONAL ORGANIZATION: BUILDING TRUST WITH TRANSPARENCY AND PERSISTENCE

1. Jim Garamone, "Diversity, Equity, Inclusion Are Necessities in U.S. Military," DOD News, February 9, 2022, https://www.defense.gov/News/News-Stories/Article/Article/2929658/diversity-equity-inclusion-are-necessities-in-us-military/
2. "Secretary General's Annual Report 2013," NATO, January 27, 2014, Updated: January 29, 2015, https://www.nato.int/cps/en/natohq/opinions_106247.htm
3. "U.S.-India Joint Statement." The White House, Office of the Press Secretary, September 30, 2014, https://obamawhitehouse.archives.gov/the-press-office/2014/09/30/us-India-joint-statement
4. "U.S.-Japan Joint Statement: The United States and Japan: Shaping the Future of the Asia-Pacific and Beyond," The White House, Office of the Press Secretary, April 25, 2014, https://obamawhitehouse.archives.gov/the-press-office/2014/04/25/us-japan-joint-statement-united-states-and-japan-shaping-future-asia-pac

CHAPTER 4: DOING THE RIGHT THING

1. "Air Force Cadet Wing Honor Code Reference Handbook," USAFA, April 27, 2022, https://www.usafa.edu/app/uploads/AFCW-Honor-Code-Handbook-27-Apr-22.pdf
2. "The Proud Legacy of the Buffalo Soldiers," National Museum of African American History and Culture, https://nmaahc.si.edu/explore/stories/proud-legacy-buffalo-soldiers

CHAPTER 7: COMING IN SECOND IS LOSING

1. "United States Air Force Weapons School," Nellis Air Force Base, November 2022, https://www.nellis.af.mil/About/Fact-Sheets/Display/Article/284156/united-states-air-force-weapons-school/#:~:text=The%20USAF%20Weapons%20School %20teaches,in %20demanding%20combat%20training%20missions

CHAPTER 9: SCHEDULE YOUR PRIORITIES

1. Senior Airman Franklin R. Ramos, "36th Fighter Squadron Celebrates a Century in the Sky," USINDOPACOM, July 25, 2017, https://www.pacom.mil/Media/News/News-Article-View/Article/1257846/36th-fighter-squadron-celebrates-a-century-in-the-sky/
2. "The P-80 Redefines 'Fast' – In the Air and On the Assembly Line," Lockheed Martin, https://www.lockheedmartin.com/en-us/news/features/history/p80.html
3. The Word "BRAT", Brats Without Borders, https://www.bratswithoutborders.org/the-word-brat

CHAPTER 14: LEADERSHIP BOLDFACE

1. Larry Brown, "Fly Like a Fighter: Emergency Procedures," AOPA, June 12, 2013, https://www.aopa.org/news-and-media/all-news/2013/june/12/critical-knowledge-emergency-checklists

CHAPTER 20: GROWING YOUR SEED CORN

1. Cornell University, http://www.gardening.cornell.edu/homegardening/scene05f6 .html

PHOTOS

MAJ GEN LARRY MARTIN

Figure 1-1: "A C-130 Hercules aircraft makes a Low-Altitude Parachute Extraction System (LAPES) supply drop at Jo Ju Air Strip during the joint Korean/U.S. Exercise Team Spirit '89," January 1, 1989, https://catalog.archives.gov/id/644825 6
Figure 1-2: "Guardian, Airman, Soldier: Two Generations," personal photo, December 13, 2020
Figure 1-3: "20070809-C 130 crew after mission in Iraq.jpg.," personal photo, August 2007
Figure 1-4: "20100302 100301-F-6213J-028 Martin Tinker Elementary with Children," https://www.macdill.af.mil/News/Photos/igphoto/2000389453/

MAJ GEN H.D. "JAKE" POLUMBO

Figure 2-1: Department of Defense, Shaw Air Force Base, South Carolina, 2015
Figure 2-2: Department of Defense, Kandahar Air Base, southern Afghanistan, 2012
Figure 2-3: Personal photo, Al Dhafra Air Base, UAE, 2009
Figure 2-4: Department of Defense, Jalalabad, eastern Afghanistan, 2013

MAJ GEN CHAD FRANKS

Figure 3-1: Personal photo, Balad Air Base, Iraq, 2007
Figure 3-2: Personal photo, Baghdad, Iraq, 2018
Figure 3-3: Personal photo, Syria/Iraq border, 2019
Figure 3-4: Air Force Maj. Gen. Chad P. Franks, 15th Air Force commander, poses in front of a MH-60G Pave Hawk after completing the helicopter's retirement flight to Hurlburt Field, Fla., May 5.; 2021 (U.S. Air Force Photo by Senior Airman Robyn Hunsinger)

MAJ GEN ROB POLUMBO

Figure 4-1: USAFA Staff, U.S. Air Force Academy, 1984
Figure 4-2: Personal photo, 2008
Figure 4-3: Personal photo, 2008
Figure 4-4: Personal photo, 2017

Made in the USA
Columbia, SC
24 February 2023

12915614R00113